The Power Before Thought

10 COMPELLING WAYS TO MANIFEST ABUNDANCE, MAGIC AND MIRACLES IN YOUR LIFE

The
Power Before
Thought

10 COMPELLING WAYS TO MANIFEST ABUNDANCE, MAGIC AND MIRACLES IN YOUR LIFE

Nigel R. Taylor

There is a thing inherent and natural,
which existed before heaven and earth.
It is motionless and fathomless.
It stands alone and never changes;
it pervades everywhere and never becomes exhausted.
It may be regarded as the Mother of the Universe.
I do not know its name;
if I am forced to give it a name, I will call it Tao,
and I name it Supreme.

LAO-TZU

DEDICATION

This book is dedicated to the Light resident in the hearts of all. May we collectively awaken from our slumber, and allow the passage of Supreme Love to permeate our beings.

Also by Nigel R. Taylor

Initiation Into Miracles
Secrets From The Master's Heart
Swami Travels In The Ocean

Edited by: Regina C. Taylor
Cover Design: Vikiana
Printed & Bound in the USA
ISBN 13-978-1500809911

CONTENTS

INTRODUCTION

If you are reading this page then it truly is time to act. This book is not designed to be average, nor is it meant to support existing viewpoints. Rather, it has been created to act as a catalyst through which you may propel yourself out of the world of our everyday *Mass Cultural Hypnosis* and into a world of magnificent possibilities. The latter world requires that you take action - now. Such action rewrites the template of your Being. It will renegotiate any relationship you may currently have to the role of being in a state of acceptance of what may *appear* to be a reality of limitation.

This book is an exploration of an opportunity for radical, unprecedented change. A Way of transmutation. A state of change in which your world no longer plays second fiddle to the whims and dying fortunes of an age that has passed. If you are truly ready to explore a world of infinite possibility, now is your chance. I challenge each of you to unlock your mindset and loosen, rather than tighten, your seat belts. No more holding on. It is a time of breathing again, a time of living rather than existing.

Nothing presented in this small book is a fact. For if something is presented as fact then it simply is not true, as you will soon see. Everything presented is a possibility. Hold close to your heart this opportunity to explore new and broader dimensions. There are infinite opportunities before us that enable us to joyfully dismiss the limited and restrictive nature of creation that has been presented to us though the time frame of the past. *All* is possible.

The pathway is before us and the cosmic chart is unfolding, moment by moment. It points us to that possibility we could never have conceived of. It is an infinite expanse of great brilliance in all facets of being, one that preempts the thought of its own existence. Getting there is the magic and mystery of our human incarnation. Being there is beyond expectation! Knowing the mystical potency, the magical power, and the joyful experience of actually being there is well worth your commitment to take the journey we explore in this volume. Moment by moment your life will become richer and deeper, and you will become more immersed in all that life truly has to offer. This life is fed by that which is *The Power Before Thought*. If you are ready and willing, let us now seek that Power.

1

A Matter Of Being

1

A Dream

"To be yourself in a world that is constantly trying to make you something else is the greatest accomplishment."
Ralph Waldo Emerson

Life is a Dream. Not just any dream, but your Dream. How you create, manifest and explore it is entirely up to you. To think otherwise is to dissolve into the lower depths of the human experience. A simple way of explaining this Dream comes from indigenous Australian Aborigines. In their reality everything is a Dream. For the Dream to exist there must be a Dreamer. The Dreamer dreams the Dream into being. Since we are all part of the Dream, the Dreamer also dreams us into existence. Within each of us is the Power of the Dream. With this Power we can dream our way back to the Dreamer. In this instance, the "Dreamer" suffices as a less complex word to explain the Source of all that is: The Godhead, the creative fount from which all pours forth. Like all dreams that we experience, the Dream is constructed of images, feelings, emotions, and perceptions. None is stuck, rigid, or unchangeable. Not one.

The opportunity for us to embrace this ancient understanding is timely. We have collectively passed through a window of linear

4

time that presented to the world one aspect of a mythology known as the tradition of the *Maya*. Much has been spoken of and written about this window. While much of this tradition has been greatly misrepresented and could comprise a book unto itself, our purposes here require but a glimpse into the meaning of the word Maya.

ENGINEERS OF THE GREATER GOOD

Maya is a Sanskrit (classical language of ancient India) word that beautifully describes our relationship to life. It may be translated as, "One who is an architect of the elements. One who can engineer thoughts into a structure." This process is the very manner in which we build and design the Dream we live in. Our unique quality as human beings is the gift of being able to engineer, design, and build our very own Dream. This is done through our faculties of imagination and visualization. Yet both of these faculties are subservient to *who we are*. You are not the slave of your imagination or your visualizations. Equally so, let me say clearly for all to hear, "You are not the slave of any one else's Dream!" Realization of this point of knowing is actually realization of *Self Knowing*; of knowing who and what you truly are in the grand cosmic scheme.

Throughout what we know as time, humanity has used its power to control the Dream in order to master a collective direction for all to follow; for individuals to align themselves with a "greater good". This greater good, however, is not always in the Greater Good. Understanding this is of paramount importance to our exploration together. That there is a Greater Good is almost universally accepted. That we are living it now and have been for the past few thousand years is, however, equally almost universally disputable. The universal or Greater Good needs some qualification. What it is and how we relate to it requires some "thought".

The idea of a Greater Good implies that there is something worthwhile to which humanity might aspire. This might be represented by a series of *idea(l)s*, and tenets to live by, such as peace, non-violence, love, truth and righteousness (much different, it should be noted, from self-righteousness). If these *idea(l)s* were consistently upheld humanity would, regardless of race, creed or culture, continually seek to engineer a Dream that would move us closer to, rather than further away from, the manifestation of greater possibilities for all.

PEACE AND NON-VIOLENCE

A cursory reflection on the past few hundred years reveals that humanity's pursuit of the Greater Good has actually been quite questionable. The Dream has been replete with wars large and small, tribal through to global, and all motivated by the idea of separation within the Dream; the idea that you and I are separate. Given that war is violent in all its forms since it creates and engineers harm physically, emotionally, mentally or spiritually to another, we can see clearly that we have collectively moved towards violence rather than non-violence. Application of the ideal of non-violence would require us to see all our actions in context of the Greater Good and eliminate any thought that would create an energy within the Dream that could hurt another. The hidden truth of this principle of non-violence is that anything that hurts another actually hurts the one who initiated the energy as well.

LOVE

Love is present in the Dream but it is tainted. Energies ranging from the slightly impure to indifference to outright hatred overshadow Love. The Dream is a mirror of the manner in which Love is made manifest. Mountains of literature have been written about unconditional love, yet very little has been written about that which is an even higher form of love. There is good reason for this. This higher love has not been actively expressed within the Dream...YET! The good news is that we can actively bring it forth within the Dream if you and I choose to, and we follow through by acting here and now.

TRUTH

Truth, always subject to scrutiny, is carefully manufactured within the Dream to keep Souls actively engaged in debate about what can be called "lesser truths". The higher Truth escapes the Dream for very few engage it. We choose not to uphold higher Truth for fear that doing so would create a collective dissolution of what we believe to be real in the Dream. It would not, however, for higher Truth is the Source Point of the Dream.

RIGHTEOUSNESS

Simply stated, Righteousness involves mindful collective action in line with the pursuit of a Greater Good. By taking actions to create in accord with Truth, Love, Non-Violence and Peace, you act with Righteousness. Understandably, a worthy ideal to engineer and manifest in your Dream.

WHAT'S THE HITCH?

Why, we might ask, does an idyllic Dream not manifest, if these ideals are worthy and are proven to engineer a Greater Good for one and all? Why are they not followed to the letter and leading us all to live in moment by moment bliss? The short version of an answer is simple. We are not living the Dream to its infinite potential because humanity operates at a lower spectrum of thought. *We create ideals and aspects of the Dream which support individuals and groups within the Dream that we have, ourselves, simultaneously created to serve the function of influencing us to create in accord with lesser truth and lesser thoughts.* Get it!? Think about it. It sounds more complex than it is. We have created the less than idyllic Dream we experience as our reality because we, ourselves, have created the Mass Cultural Hypnosis that veils Truth and the Greater Good. Why then, you are now thinking, have we created the less than idyllic individuals and institutions that serve to "bind" us to the lesser truths and lesser thoughts and lesser reality we live as our Dream. What purpose does that serve?! Let's see.

As we have just established, the "Lords and Masters" within the Dream that we find ourselves subservient to are our own creation. Why do they exist? *Because they assist us to avoid looking at a deeper Truth.* They are our insurance agents. They manage the risk and assets of our life in accord with the way we have collectively decided they should.

Through them we are able to project our thoughts and the resulting realities created outside ourselves. Rather than reflect inwardly upon our thoughts and actions and realize that we ourselves are the genesis of these thoughts, we project them outward and manifest all manner of creation as "separate" from ourselves, or outside ourselves. This reinforces the established ideal of separation, so strong in human understanding, which in turn brings forth "you and me", rather than "one", and judgment of one against another. Such judgments then facilitate the full spectrum of envy, jealousy, anger, rage and so forth. These in turn fill the trough from which violence and all other societal ills feed. Through separation and the support of "oppressive" ideals and entities, humanity supports the arguments active within the Dream that keep us collectively on guard against the true nature of our existence and what it means to be human. These arguments can then be engineered to heavily favor outward projections of what can be termed "benchmarks" in linear time. Very convenient.

These benchmarks are well-known focus points such as "the end of the world" markers of Y2K or December 21st, 2012. There have been infinite others which similarly prove the following point: We set up the markers, work towards them, pass through them, and yet...you got it...we are still here! This is the power of Mass Cultural Hypnosis. It is a cultural and societal engineering of the Dream that keeps us in the dark as to our true nature. It is a field of energy that propagates fear. When enough aspects of our being attribute value to this benchmark, consciously or subconsciously, then it has achieved its purpose - the fear of the extinction of physical reality: The great unknown and detachment from all that we believe is of value inside the Dream. This applies

8

for one and all, including all who think they are "beyond it", "above it", "detached from it", or "in surrender". The Dream is the Dream is the Dream.

The Human Experience

"When ever you find yourself on the side of the majority,
it is time to pause and reflect."
Mark Twain

We can see clearly now that we live inside a Dream that we create. While this is really no great secret, it is a knowing that helps us to gain Self-understanding. The question that now begs to be answered is, "What is it to be human?" This is an age-old question and one that has been answered in innumerable ways. During one of the seminars I recently conducted I asked our group, "What is it to be human? What specifically defines a human being?" I received a variety of responses, most of which one would have predicted. Here are some of them. They said, "Humans...

    * Are physical beings with a body, mind and Soul
    * Are divine
    * Eat, sleep, drink and sustain themselves through the five elements
    * Relate to each other
    * Have personality
    * Are cultural beings."

The list displays our tendency to fall into the matrix of common thought patterns. At this point I will share a sweet anecdote from the early part of my life to highlight the obvious.

COME BARK OR COME BITE...

During the 1960's and 70's I held a weekend and summer job as a postman in Perth, Western Australia, my hometown and state. I was attending university so this work helped to pay some bills. Each day I would arrive on my bicycle at one particular house to deliver the mail. And each day, from the depths of Dante's Inferno, appeared a dog (beast), roaring out of the shadows, teeth shining, and making sounds befitting the final moments of the Sirens. He would grab hold of my shoe and not let go until I could shake him off with great effort. It was a harrowing experience.

My chosen solution to this daily attack was to drop the whole street's mail in the first mailbox in the street and hightail out of the place. Using this tactic I managed to avoid confronting the little blighter entirely. Eventually, however, the folks at the beginning of the street had had quite enough of delivering everyone else's mail and thus reported the matter to the postmaster. A visit by the postmaster sorted it all out. The next day, upon assurance of the postmaster, I approached the house and awaited my fate. The owner had taken the day off work to be there when I arrived. Out came the dog, teeth shining in open disdain, and he ran at me like there was no tomorrow. Though growling, snarling, and offensively cornering me, he cleverly chose to not bite me in the presence of his master. The owner instructed me to pick him up and place him in the carry basket at the front of my bike where all the mail was kept. After considerable and heated discussion, I reluctantly followed her instructions.

Immediately, the dog stopped growling and proceeded to sit in the bag with a self-satisfied expression as he observed with interest the goings-on along the rest of the street. It soon became clear that all he really wanted was to ride in my bike basket and survey his territory from a greater height. You see, he had it all worked out. There were a couple of Dobermans that lived at the end of the street. They were contained by a waist-high picket fence, so he could not approach them and exclaim his superiority from the ground level. He needed a position of height to announce his victory! Once we had passed the Dobermans he hopped off the bike and, with an almost witty smile, paced back to his home. All he truly desired was a nice ride and the ability to survey his territory. He just had a very bad way of expressing his desires. Apparently, he had employed this tactic successfully for years to elicit the help of the previous postman, until I inherited his route. His rather gruff manner of informing me was simply due to a personality disorder. After all, he was a Silky Terrier and all of a foot long and six inches off the ground.

In addition to providing a good story, my little friend helps to illustrate a point for us in light of our query into what it means to be human. After relaying this story to the group, I pointed out that dogs fulfill all of the above qualities they had provided to define what it is to be human - and many more.

WHO ARE WE REALLY?

Hence, I asked again, "What is it to be human?" It is not "the personality" as someone suggested. My little friend certainly had that. A personality is a matrix of beliefs, attitudes and dispositions we collect around ourselves to help us define our relationship to the Dream. Our personality is not born with us. For while I do not dispute the relevance within the Dream of Astrology, Numerology, Gematria and all the derivatives thereof, I do make the case that they are not our masters unless we *make* them our masters. There is great truth in each of these branches of metaphysical study. However, they are not the highest Truth to which we can aspire. They exist within the Dream. They do not come *before* the thought of the Dream. Consider here how the law of gravity states unequivocally that we cannot fly, and yet the law of aerodynamics reveals that the former law can be both overcome and made obsolete. Above and beyond this, the Dream contains infinite higher laws as yet not even contemplated. They are awaiting our deep, heartfelt exploration of the Dream for their unfolding.

YOUR LIFE IN ACTION

It would be equally incorrect to stipulate that we are born tied to
our karma. We can understand and accept the principle of karma
at the level of the Dream but not subscribe to it as a limiting factor
in our incarnation. Karma simply means "action". Actions are
always precipitated by thought, and thought is sourced in the
highest reaches of consciousness. Not all thoughts are directly
precipitated by one's own Soul, but rather are precipitated by
other parts of ourselves within the Dream. Hence as a servant
of the greater Dream one may be subservient to the actions of
previous incarnations. That in turn brings up another whole
arena for contemplation - and this relates to our knowing of time.
We will explore that strand in the web of Truth later, but suffice
it to say that when we explore this issue, *actions as karma* will
take on a whole new meaning. The advice to be gleaned here is to
not become too attached to your karma or your personality. As
masters of the Dream we are not limited by the lower vibrations
of karma. All we need do is master how to rise above them. This,
of course, is entirely possible, given that karma is part of the
Dream as well. Both our group in class and you as the dreamer
understand that while all of these considerations are part of the
Dream, none defines what it means to be human. What then is our
answer? Slowly our awareness now grasps the principle of Truth at
the core of our "human-ness".

SELF-REFLECTIVE CONSCIOUSNESS

We have within us a quality that can be defined as "Self-Reflective
Consciousness". This is part of the Dream and does not exist
outside the Dream. Within the Dream it is a leading indicator of
how we may break through the limits of the Dream and, in so
doing, rise above them. The "Self" part of this principle of being
human is about the knowing that we are both *in* the Dream and
above the Dream. The "Reflective" part is the Self's knowing that

everything we experience around us is but a reflection within the Dream of our own Self. With awareness of this quality intact we move closer to understanding what it is to be human.

THE HUMAN AND THE BEING

For aeons humans have separated the *Human* from the *Being*. The Human is the physical-personality driven, mind-centered, emotional and mentally constructed aspect of individual consciousness within the Dream. This part has a matrix of existence that is constantly changing, dynamic and forever relating to multi-dimensional aspects of the infinite universes that exist.

The Being part, however, is the key to knowing who we truly are. The changing human is dynamic and caught up in projections and reflections. The Being is changeless, at peace, non-violent, righteous, and truthful. The vital element in this equation that must be understood and lit with bright neon is as follows. *The Being is, in essence, existent in the Dream and also before the Thought of the Dream.* For the being there is no movement, no evolution, no growth and no unfolding. This part simply is. What we today call the "Human Being" has gotten caught up in the rigid, lower-level vibratory belief that we are Human, rather than the Being that is driving the former into a space of higher grandeur. The Power Before Thought acts directly through the Being before that which we think of as the human. And contrary to the assumptions of the lesser Dream, it is in fact the Being that is driving the lesser aspects of our humanness towards perfection, not our humanness that drives us to the higher state.

Why? The lower vibrational part of our humanness is a composite of the elements of the Dream: earth, water, fire, air and spirit. All of these are sentient and provide us with the raw material through which we construct the Dream. These are the tools of Maya. These are the materials through which we, in our Beingness, construct individual and collective thoughtforms. It is through these raw materials that we become who we *believe* we are. Or, put another way, it is through these elements that we become who others (those who we have created in our Dream) have told us we are. It is for us to choose: *It is for us to choose who we dream ourselves to be: Humans of Mass Cultural Hypnosis or Beings of Truth timelessly existent as The Power Before Thought.*

The good news is that we are not helpless, static and subject to the rules of a Human-designed game. Rather we are potent creative aspects of One Being. It is the manner in which this Power is actuated and brought into fullness that determines how and what we manifest in our lives and, as a result, for the Greater Good.

3

Everything Is A Suggestion

"Life isn't about finding yourself. Life is about creating yourself."
George Bernard Shaw

Life is one big possibility. It is a suggestion to participate in the Dream and manifest an abundance of opportunities, all of which are latent inside our beings. Our challenge is to understand what it is to be Human, and the nature of our Being, in the context of this abundance. To do so it pays us to consider another very simple question. "What is real and what is not real?"

When you arise each and every morning to start your new day, you do so based on a series of assumptions. Namely, the assumption made when you retire at night that you will indeed awaken in the morning to continue your sojourn in this dimension; the assumption that you will have the same body, no doubt the same health, and the same life partner and/or family; the assumption that you will awaken within the same framework of cultural norms; the assumption that you will know who you are; and last, but not least, the assumption that your bed will still be there.

THOUGHTFORMS MADE MANIFEST

All of these assumptions reflect no more and no less than a relationship your personality has with your thoughtforms. Follow carefully here. Everything in the Dream is a thoughtform. Everything! Consider the following example. A team of specialists, using the principles of engineering, architecturally designed the Empire State Building. First, however, the idea was conceived of in the mind of one or more individuals. As a thought it became manifest. As a building it certainly appears solid and encourages us to believe we are safe and secure inside its structure. However, it is a composite of the five elements of earth, water, fire, air, and spirit. If we take any of these down to its base level we find that we will eventually "arrive" at molecular structure and then beyond into the field of energy. The Empire State Building is a field of energy. There is nothing new in this observation, yet here is a twist. The Empire State Building is held together in your Dream by your support for its existence. If you collapse your Dream and rewrite the codes, you leave this third dimensional reality behind - and with it the Empire State Building itself.

The same can be said for everything in your Dream. Your house, car, clothing, food, terror threats, and so forth. Everything exists because you have assigned value to it inside your Dream. You have accepted, at the level of personality, a structural meaning behind the purpose of each element of your Dream. You live through the existence of each element as part of the whole - with a stronger relationship to some elements than to others. Everything is a thoughtform to the personality. These examples represent the physical structures of the Dream, but the same principle applies for the non-physical thought projections in our Dream. Our feelings and emotions that are at the foundation of our interaction with our self and others are also thoughtforms. The idea (Maya, or Dream construct) that a person is trustworthy, for example, is a thoughtform, as also is the idea that you may yourself be successful or failing in some aspect of the Dream.

Exploring this a step further, we find that we must consider what quantum physics tells us about reality. In a nutshell it tells us that nothing exists unless we effectively *will* it to exist. In other words, something exists because we have, through the act of observation, collapsed a series of frequencies (which in themselves are part of the Dream) into reality. In other words, a thoughtform - or architectural possibility – to be made manifest only exists when we choose to manifest it. This is when we really start to scratch our heads in wonder and ask an obvious question. "If thoughtforms require the force of will to be made manifest, why do we experience so many things that we have simply never conceived of in any conscious way?" Not to mention those things that we would never choose, at the level of personality, to bring into existence! Herein lies the rub. Herein also lies a very meaningful moment of discovery and deep understanding. Ready?

The Mass Cultural Hypnosis in the Dream of humanity is a constant field of pulsating constructs. This field of Mass Cultural Hypnosis serves the higher master energies that seek to project a lesser Dream into the collective consciousness. This lesser Dream, as we have illustrated earlier, is one of subservience, limitation and constraint - in all its varied forms. It is all that a higher Dream, supported through the ideals of Peace, Non-Violence, Love, Truth, and Righteousness for the Greater Good, is not. Yet, as we have also seen, despite the great control wielded through Mass Cultural Hypnosis, the lesser Dream is still *our* Dream and is always, in truth, under our control. The reason it appears to *not* be so much in our control reflects the fact that the lesser Dream is well constructed and choreographed to best suit the collective unfolding of who and what we are.

The Power before the Thought of the Dream that we are, in pursuit of bringing to us Self-knowing as a Human Being, orchestrates scenarios through which we can grow and learn and evolve! There is a great power at work moving this Dream forward, constantly constructing these scenarios, many of which we vehemently declare we do not like or support. Some scenarios play out to influence our lower self, or personality existence, and others play out to direct, cultivate and heal our higher Self from lower vibrational attachments.

THE REAL AND THE UNREAL

If we just accept (for fun) that everything is a thoughtform and that all thoughtforms are possibilities, and that all possibilities are no more than suggestions - some of which are from our higher Self and others from the lower aspects of self, let us then again ask, "What is real and what is unreal?" When you retire at night and go to sleep, where does the bed go? Think about this for a moment. Where does it go? It is certainly not in your dream, unless you are half awake and half asleep. When you are asleep where does it go? It is a suggestion. It exists because you will it to be, and equally so it ceases to exist because you will it to cease to exist. When you dream, you do so by shifting a series of functions at a physical level. This in turn engages the higher dimensional aspects of your Being to release the attachment to the lower vibrational thoughtforms and structures of linear time-based reality. When you awaken the bed is there, but why? Why is it there? It is there because you expect it to be there, and this expectation is built upon past evidence. Past evidence is based upon memories. Memories are visualizations and projections of thoughtforms into time and space that are actually beyond time and space. In other words, every morning you create the Dream anew. This is true for every aspect of reality that you experience in this lower vibrational dimension of the Dream.

It is time for another anecdote to reinforce the significance of these insights into the Dream. Part of my journey in this life is to act as an instrument to assist people to "heal". I will address in a deeper sense the meaning of healing shortly, but suffice it to say that clients come to me for this interaction. During the process many different experiences unfold, but there is one in particular that relates to what we are exploring in context of thoughtforms and the Dream.

BE CAREFUL WHAT YOU DREAM OF!

One day I was working in session with my client Joan (a fictitious name). Joan was standing quietly next to me as I interacted with her personality, Spirit and the many dimensional aspects of the Dream that she had created. While looking through the window of time and space (which is possible for all of us), I noticed a small brown dog had been brought forth in Spirit. I asked Joan if she and her family had a dog. She answered that they did not. The dog persisted, and so I asked her if she was *sure* that she had not had a dog (as if she would not remember having a dog!) The answer again was, "No, no dog." Following the prompting that persisted from Spirit, I asked one more time. At this point Joan broke into heartfelt laughter. It took her a while to regain her composure. When she did, what unfolded offers a very important insight to all of us.

Joan revealed that she had never actually had a dog growing up, but that during childhood her family had dearly wanted one. Circumstances of finance and other issues prevented them from having one. The solution adopted by the entire family was to create an imaginary dog, which they did. Joan explained that she, along with her parents and siblings, had created an imaginary dog which they "kept" throughout her childhood and beyond. They fed it, played with it, put it to bed, nurtured it, and loved it, for many, many years. This dog that was in their imagination - and so real to them in their minds - was now re-presenting itself to her at a time of healing.

Why her dog re-presented itself is part of Joan's Soul journey, but for the rest of us the lesson for our own journeys is most clear. Everything we imagine within our consciousness is created. Every thought has power. And so I ask you, *"What are your dogs that track you through the dimensions? Are they pets of yours? Are they happy and joyful? Do they provide an abundance of opportunity to play in the fields of your Dream? Or are they demons that chase you through the corridors of time and space? Are they constantly reminding and re-creating blocks and challenges to the greater achievements of the*

Self?" The gift offered to all of us by Joan's little dog is certainly one to be cherished.

The key to each and every one of our "next moments" is to know that the dog is as real as the bed. When our focus shifts from one dimension of the Dream to another, so also shifts the imposition of our thoughtforms upon the free flow of our Beingness. What then is real and what is not? Who are you? What are you? All these questions follow us on our journey and in so doing provide us with great opportunities to reclaim an abundance of love, light, and joy into our world and our Dream.

4

$\mathcal{B}eing$

"Knowing yourself is the beginning of all wisdom."
Aristotle

Within the Vedic Tradition of ancient India and the sacred text, Brhadaranyaka Upanishad, (*Bri-huh-thaa-ruh-nyuh-kuh Oop-ah-knee-shad*) can be found a very powerful mantra. It reads very simply and yet its import is deep and profound. It serves us well in our exploration. You need not worry about how to pronounce it or sing it; I have included the Sanskrit wording simply to reveal its essence.

Asato Maa Sad-Gamaya
Tamaso Maa Jyotir-Gamaya
Mrtyor-Maa Amrtam Gambia
Om Shanti Shanti Shanti

Lead us from *Unreality* (of Transitory Existence)
to the *Reality* (of Self),
Lead us from the *Darkness* (of Ignorance)
to the *Light* (of Spiritual Knowledge),
Lead us from the Fear of *Death*
to the Knowledge of *Immortality*.
Om Peace, Peace, Peace

This prayer is an appeal to the Highest Source to lead us from Unreality to Reality. The mantra begs us to deepen our search into the question of what is real and what is unreal and reveals also the essence of the Self as Immortal. Pure Light. It is a sound toning, with an intent that seeks to shift our Dream from the lower vibrational energies to higher ones. We have already established the unreal nature of our Dream as lower vibrational energies. We have illustrated the manner in which the Human is divorced from Being and witnessed the transient nature of life. So why then do we appear to become stuck in the "same ole same ole" way of being? Why do we repeat the same issues with financial lack, health challenges, relationship upsets and of course the global ones of war, violence etc. This is a good time to ask some deeper questions.

PHYSICAL

If I asked you whether or not you had a Physical Body, without doubt most of you would say, "Yes." My next question would then be, *"Are you your Physical Body?"* Many of you would immediately say, "No," revealing that you have been students of spiritual tradition for some time. The answer is that *yes*, you most definitely do have a Physical Body, and *no*, you are not your Physical Body. Why, therefore, do you behave as if you *are* your Physical Body? It does not pay to deny that you do, unless you are the one sole truly enlightened being on the planet. (I see your brow furrowing, because you have surely heard of all those proclaimed enlightened ones roaming the planet. Yet I would say the following in response. Many are those who will tell you they are Self-realized or enlightened. Beware the self-proclaimed, they are usually the ones with most to lose, and you do not want to be part of all that.) Again, "Why?"

Our answer is found within the Dream and the power of thoughts. Everything in the collective Dream that we create suggests - yes, suggests - to us that we are, in fact, physical beings. This suggestive power supports the memory of our previous linear time experiences, promotes future possibilities based upon those experiences, and propels us to take actions based upon expectations of those projections within the Dream. For example, the mass media is replete with advertisements that support the physical being. They may present young vibrant folks who enjoy happy, healthy, and dynamic lives: Young happy families eating all the "right foods" and doing all the "good things". Reinforcement is the key to keeping the Dream intact. (Think back to my postman story. These dogs follow us everywhere and they want a good vista on our lives!) Advertisers then project into the future to illustrate another group of folks with expectations of old age, frailty, and with the need for insurance and attendant requirements of all sorts. With all of this going on, and the cultural model of aging and retirement, the mass of humanity understandably finds it very easy to succumb to the "I am a physical being" Dream.

Images presented to us en masse by the media are, however, merely that - images. They are thoughtforms projected into your field of beingness. They are templates that we find great ease in filling, feeling comfortable with the way we fit into these templates. To illustrate how this works, let us delve into the world of Mass Cultural Hypnosis and, in particular, the highly effective field of advertising.

Let us imagine that you are watching television and on the screen appears a commercial from Ford for their new Mustang. Follow the process of what happens as you interact with this commercial. The image of the Mustang is perceived within your energy field as a car. It has colour, shape, form, and function. It may be sexy and have appeal. This image is *within* you, but you saw it, heard about it, and felt it by way of a media broadcast. What is a broadcast? The broadcast is comprised of a series of frequencies coded into a signal and projected through time and space to a satellite, by means of which it is redirected down to surround specific sectors of planet Earth. If you choose to turn on your TV and cable box, and you tune in to the respective receiver, you will experience the coded message that has been architecturally designed for you. There before you appears the commercial, decoded for you to see. When you (or any of us) bring your historical matrix of past unreality to bear in that moment, *meaning is given to this projection.* It is now real! It may generate desires, emotions and deep feelings, and this structures behavior to follow suit.

Now, look at this in context of the Greater Good. Though our Mustang may be a more benign image than many others, the Dream is a composite of infinite images, many of which pull us collectively downwards into fear. It is the rising above these images, and the fear, that is the mark of one who has unlocked and works from the sacred space of the Power before these thoughts came into being – the Power Before Thought.

The Dream that includes our Mustang has many layers. It did not just start and unfold in linear time. It has been unfolding over time and has linear time historical precedent. For prior to the broadcast, a video crew filmed the car and brought the raw material to an editor who then conceived of a way of imaging it for our mass consumption. Sound, light, background, and so forth were considered and chosen for their greatest effect. Even earlier along the track there was a decision made to create the car. The car was (just like the Empire State Building) conceived in the minds of a group of engineers (practitioners of high Maya). Going back even further there was a choice to need a car. Not this car, but any car. That choice came about from a greater need, and that need was the ability to travel with ease. Such ease of travel has had many evolutionary steps, but at the end of the day it comes back to an inner desire to make life easier in the physical domain. Somewhere in the greater ethers of the matrix, there existed (and still exists) the full spectrum of ideas that surround movement and travel. The car, and in particular this Mustang, are just evolutionary developments in the unfolding Dream.

Clearly, many of these steps forward do *enhance* the quality of the Dream, helping us rise up and away from lower vibratory thoughts. Yet others simply reaffirm the earthly, physical attachment that drives us deeper into the Dream. These become our limitations for which we argue so strongly. Recognizing and working with the Power Before Thought to dissolve these limitations, and generating instead an increase in higher vibratory thoughts within the Dream, offers us lives free of all limitation and supportive of the Greater Good.

Consistently and repeatedly we have collectively structured the Dream to suit our perceived limitations. Many of these limitations can be traced back to false awareness of our true nature. This false awareness having been programmed into us by those who knew how to control the Dream. These "Dream Masters" of the ancient past were often at odds with each other. There were those who supported the *Self* and those who saw a need to support the self. This is an ancient battle that is only today coming of age, as we shake off the chains that bind us. If you accept the images and projections you perceive as truth without question, then you will conduct your life as guided by them. *Yet they are not truth, they are suggestions.*

EMOTIONAL

You have a Physical Body; so equally do you have an Emotional Body. You have emotions. You are not, however, your emotions. There are many who believe that they are their emotions, but in believing and acting as if they are, they limit the reality of their Being. It is unreal to become invested in emotions. You are not your anger, hurt, pain, suffering, greed, envy, jealousy, lust, fears, or resentments. Nor are you your loves, joys, appreciations, happiness, and so forth. All of these are still projections within the field of the personality. The media does a good job at manipulating these projections and bundling them into presentations of images that support an emotionally charged physical being. Society, accepting the repetitive nature of these projections, happily carries them forth to generate a greater reality tone for them. We concretize them into powerful structures. They come out in our everyday interactions of politics, religion, sport, education and everyday family affairs. Yet, they are just thoughtforms. *They are not real.*

You are not your emotions. It is possible to walk into a cloud of emotional energy and feel it at a very deep level. These feelings are not real, no matter how hard one argues for them. They simply cease to exist when you cease to exist. Your universe dissolves when you cease to exist! You are the creator of your own universe. That means all experiences of the full spectrum of emotion are being experienced *within* you. When you cease to exist, all the hurt, pain, anguish, joy, ecstasy and wonder simply dissolve back into Source. You are greater than your Physical Body, greater than your emotions, and greater than…your beliefs.

MENTAL

What are beliefs? Generally speaking they are a series of mental constructs (thoughtforms) that help us make sense of reality. Here's how it works, as seen through the lens of our exploration thus far. Reality is a Dream composed of countless thoughtforms which, though unreal, are nevertheless supported by the lower Dream. These thoughtforms are thus empowered to revivify past memories into future possibilities. This is all based upon the suggestion of permanency that we use to relate to our existence. Remember the bed? It disappears when we sleep. We all know, however, that beliefs vary from one person to another, one group to another, nation to nation, religion to religion, etc. We are not our beliefs, and yet how many times do we become so invested in our beliefs that they bring the full force of our emotional and physical beings to fight for our self-defense? This is the basis of all argument, and such argument serves to support the continuance of the unreality that we are working hard to dissolve. Do you see how much fertile ground we have laid for a deep break away from the Greater Good?

Think about it. Have you ever once become involved in an argument? If the answer is "Yes," then I congratulate you for being honest and know you will find yourself laughing as you continue reading. Have you ever become involved in an argument and half way through you realize that you are wrong? Yes? No? For most of us the answer is a definitive, "Yes!" Now, here is the clincher. Have you ever become involved in an argument and half way through you realize that you are wrong AND you keep on arguing? Part of you is saying, "This is not a good thing...bad idea...you are wrong and you know it," and yet you keep on arguing. What part is speaking to you, telling you that you should actually cease and desist? This part is known as the Observer. We will come back to this part, and all associated issues this raises, later in our exploration. This Observer is an intimate friend of the Power Before Thought.

SPIRITUAL

Thus far we have determined that you are not your Physical, Emotional, or Mental Body. You are greater than all of them, and yet you create them in order to have a vehicle through which to relate to the Dream. The other body you use to navigate your beingness is your Spiritual Body. There are many names given to each of the different aspects of Spirit such as "etheric", "causal" and "astral". Just let those be for now. They do serve a purpose, but they also support the Dream that you are moving in and through. No matter how you define your Spirit body, you are greater than that. Though some would argue to hold the limitation that they are the Spirit, I repeat that if you argue for your limitations you will truly live them to the fullest. Being greater than your Spiritual Body then poses another question. What else are you greater than?

GREATER THAN... ?

Here we go. What I am about to say may not sit well with many, many folks out there. I will say it and then we will consider it. You are greater than the greatest thought you can conceive of - and that includes God. *Yes, you are greater than God!* For atheists this will be no problem, for they sit comfortably with the understanding that there is no God. Agnostics may likely also find a degree of comfort in this, because they probably know where we are headed. The issue is not the existence or non-existence of God. The issue is the Dream and what we do inside the Dream to create and limit ourselves, and how we support ourselves to avoid detachment from the unreal. If you can define God, by any name, creed, culture, be it historical or the living God, then you have limited God. Anything you can name you have brought to the level of human personality. If God is human then God is in the Dream and limited by the Dream. Once you come to the realization that you cannot define God, the Supreme, the Ultimate, the Source, then you are able to Be all that you came here to be. The actual defining of the Supreme limits the potency of the Absolute in your life journey.

AN ILLUSION OF SEPARATION

A little hypothetical human drama will help deepen our exploration of this understanding. Let us say that three people meet. Sue, Bob, and Jane. Sue is a friend of Bob's. Jane knows neither of them before meeting Bob at a conference. Bob says something that ignites Jane's personality, causing her to feel hurt. Maybe it's an unintended sleight. Jane, however, based upon her memories of past experiences with others, takes it personally. She instantly categorizes Bob as rude, ignorant, and an undesirable person. Jane later meets Sue at the same conference. In a private discussion with Jane, Sue expresses her absolute delight at knowing such a divine Soul as Bob. Jane, in retort, expresses her deep dislike for Bob, explaining that he is not the kind of person she wishes to engage or be near - at all. Here presented are two radically different opinions of Bob. Who is right and who is wrong? Neither is right nor wrong. Trick question? Trick answer? No, there is a most helpful insight to this "trick" that reaches beyond basic psychology.

There are three points to connect to uncover this insight and reveal clearly how we are greater than our Spiritual Body. Firstly, Sue, Bob and Jane are all thoughtforms in each other's Dream. As thoughtforms they exist as possibilities. They exist because there was a specific intent to collapse a possibility, or a suggestion, into reality; their reality is the Dream.

Secondly, each interaction they have with each other is an inner world experience. A composite of emotions, feelings and attitudes are playing through as a series of set rules by which judgments are brought to the surface in the Dream. All these judgments are fostered and supported by the Mass Cultural Hypnosis that has brought us to this point in our human experience.

Thirdly, and most importantly, is the passing of judgment. It serves us to employ here the use of an oft-quoted commandment: "Thou shalt not judge." Stay with me now, I'm not going to start preaching! There is a good reason for the application of this phrase, and it does not harken back to a literal Biblical projection. In effect, when Jane expresses her dislike of Bob, she diminishes herself, because Bob is her own creation. Likewise, when Sue expresses her delight at having Bob in her life, she expands her self. One diminishes and the other expands, yet both are judging the same person? Not so. *Both are dealing with and judging their own projections, and in so doing they are judging themselves.*

JUDGMENT GOES VIRAL

Let us now consider how this personal act of judging and limiting through the application of our hard-fought-for thoughtforms and beliefs plays out in the grander scheme of things. A Christian judges a Moslem, A Moslem judges a Jew, a Black judges a White, an Atheist judges a Believer, or vice versa: The list of these judgments could go on ad infinitum. The judgments are, in and of themselves, part of Maya, or the Dream, and they are encouraged to exist and continue. The encouragement for their continual existence is found in the field of the media (in all its modalities), in our daily discussions, and in the images and sounds that fill our Dream on a daily basis. Simply think of politics, religion, or sports and you have the gist of it. If we truly want to change our world, to experience the richness and fullness of life, then this is a key of great importance to us as we take our journey. *Whenever we diminish another in our own eyes, we diminish ourselves.*

To uplift, praise, and expand another is to grant life, love and evolutionary wisdom to another. We are greater than all of our Physical, Emotional, Mental, Spiritual bodies, and we are greater than all known and unknown realities that we portray as absolutes. Even as we look upon those who appear to be portraying deep and dark behavior we must always remember that they are part of our Dream. We must transform ourselves in order for these parts to heal. They are the dogs that follow us around wherever we go. Remember, when you cease to exist in time and space so do all of your problems, goals, judgments, and joys. You are the creator of your own Universe.

11

Beyond The Boundaries
Of Time

What Serves Your Expansion

"The Truth." Dumbledore sighed. "It is a beautiful and terrible thing,
and should be treated with great caution."
J.K. Rowling

Our emphasis in this unfolding journey is expansion. Expansion is life. Contraction is death. To seek to expand one's horizon within the Dream, to reach deeply into the Dream while simultaneously yearning to break through the Dream - and experience the Power Before Thought - is the ultimate quest of the *HeartSpace Warrior.* To advance our quest, it is timely to unravel the mysteries of beingness more fully. This is our Self-reflective quality coming to our rescue!

Accepting the fundamentals of leading edge quantum physics as our beacon, we can fairly comfortably state that everything is a possibility; everything is a suggestion; everything is a frequency; everything is light. Not light in the sense of daylight or artificial light. Light in this sense refers to dimensions of beingness, the densest of which, in the human experience, is the Physical Body. The least dense dimension, in the human experience, cannot be named, for to do so defines and limits it. Hence we are on a journey from a solid Dream, thoughtform dictated and structured by the engineers and architects of Maya, through to the dreamless state existing as the Power Before Thought. No architect exists here. Neither does individuality, which is a cause of fear for the ego and personality. There is only Unity in the state of pre-thought. What a majestic and beautiful journey, and one in which we are already deeply engrossed. The issue confronting us now is clear. How do we work with these varying levels of light within the Dream to peel back the layers and reveal this Power Before Thought in all its glory?

CAREFUL, YOUR BODY CAN HEAR YOU

Our most base level body within the Dream is our Physical Body. Understood at the level of personality, it is a composite of interrelated and interacting systems that function together synergistically. When everything in the environment is harmonious the body generally functions well. When one or more elements get out of kilter, however, things start to shift out of homeostatic balance and disease steps in. What is dis-ease?

Think of every organ, tissue, gland and cell as belonging to a greater whole. There appears to be a hierarchical relationship whereby the lower level (cells) responds to the higher level directives from the Being. Since all organs and tissues are composed of cellular structure, our interest is in understanding what makes the systems break down. If we review the work of Dr. Bruce Lipton and the study of Epigenetics, it becomes abundantly clear that our old model of understanding human biological processes is fairly outdated, if not basically wrong. Epigenetics, in a nutshell, informs us that consciousness (awareness) changes our genes - not the other way around. While this is no big surprise to many, it does go straight to the core of our modern day dogma that defines us to be genetically pre-determined and therefore subject to the whims of our ancestral lineage through codings passed down by parental DNA.

Since consciousness is the key here, and since all of this is taking place inside the Dream, let us explore the relationship among the differing levels of Being. For a start, the Physical Body is subservient to the Emotional Body in a hierarchical sense. Emotions dictate directives to the Physical Body. The Physical Body makes adaptations to the emotional energetic imprints that are timelessly passed on to the coding structures within the cellular core - or DNA. Sufficient emotional disharmony will lead to major adaptations at a physical level. These adaptations can, for instance, be observed in the energy field of a client who comes for healing. Emotions are precursors to either health and well being or to disease states. This is ancient spiritual healing wisdom. It crosses all known barriers and holds true regardless of where one is placed inside the Dream. Over the past thirty years this has been insightfully portrayed through the work of Louise Hay and her small book titled, *The Body Can Heal Itself.*

Hay's premise, by no means new, yet succinctly expressed, is that for every single disease condition there is a direct correlation with the world of thought and language. Or, as we would say here, wherever the body is out of harmony within the greater Dream there is a thought process that underlies it. The powerful tool utilized by Hay is greatly misunderstood and/or simply decried because of its simplicity. She engages the area of the body and explores the disease. Once there she tracks across to a cause and ultimately highlights the negative thinking involved. Part of her solution is to substitute what we would deem a negative thought process, expressed through less than positive language, with positive language. This positive language is uplifting and healing. It all sounds almost too simple if simply taken at face value, yet there is enormous depth to this art. To explore these concepts even superficially you may feel you want to keep your seat belt fastened. In so doing, as always, remember that all I share is a suggestion inside the Dream. A *suggestion*, albeit one that assists us move comfortably through the lower vibrational Dream and into the infinite Power Before Thought.

POWER OF SACRED WORD AND SYMBOL

At the physical level, human beings communicate with each other through a complex interaction of speech and body language. That there are much higher levels of communication is indisputable, but we are not yet ready to go there at this point in our exploration. Let us therefore ask another question: "What is speech?" Speech is a complex series of utterances expressing some inner world dialogue, perception or realization that is taking place inside the broadcaster. These utterances are, in our modern world, structured of language derived from alphabets composed of letters. All languages have their own grammatical rules and attributes that distinctly define and differentiate them from one another, i.e. Latin from Hindi. If we dig below the surface of the world's languages, we enter the realm of ancient sacred scriptures and the teachings of Mystery Schools. Once inside these realms we are led to understand that each and every letter is a sacred portal in and of itself. By "portal" we mean that each letter is an opening to higher-level dimensional realities, experiences and realizations than those we have in everyday existence.

II

Beyond the
Boundaries of Time

Use and management of these sacred alphabets is such that in ancient times initiates were trained in mastery of their pronunciation. Intonation and evocation of these sounds were of vital importance. These sacred letters were so revered that each one of them was, in some way, linked to a god or goddess energy, or to some other greatly important spiritual frequency resident in the higher dimensions. When specific letters were correctly articulated together, the door to higher realms was opened. Put together, a string of these sacred letters would create something even more powerful - an energy field of multiple frequencies that became alive within the Dream. Hence gods and goddesses were summoned forth, as were also demons and darkness. There is much that can be said relative to this, but here and now is not the place or time. This is a very powerful subject and yet, for our purposes, currently remains a suggestion.

As linear time has passed language has become very basic.

People speak in a new language everyday. Computer speak, emoticons, texting and the like reign in modern culture. This brings us back to Hay's premise presented earlier. When people have an inner dialogue that is less than supportive of the Greater Good, the greater Dream, and, ultimately, the Power Before Thought, they will use language that is often demeaning, dismissive, or destructive to the higher energy field. This brings consequences to the lower vibrational Physical Body. This body is a composite of frequencies that responds to the light it receives. Language is frequency and, at the end of the day, language is light.

FIELDS OF LIGHT TAKE UP PHYSICAL RESIDENCE

A negative affirmation, such as an expression of great anger towards another, sends a consciousness imprint to the cellular structure of the receiver. It is a messenger sent to make room for the field of lower vibrational light. This field of light is anger and its place of residence will most likely become the liver. Why the liver? An infinite body of wisdom from multiple traditions, including Classical Acupuncture and Ayurveda, explains why this is so. Another example of how these fields take residence in the physical form could be a negative projection pertaining to hurt, love, loss or lack of self-love. For these fields of light, given the right conditions, the target organ will be the heart.

The organs are the receptacles of the negative aspects of the inner Dream. In the same way that shining light directly into the retina will cause the pupil to contract, so does shining the light of pain, anguish, hurt, despair, and jealousy cause their resonant organs to contract. How does dis-ease then enter? The projection of destructive fields of light, and their establishment within the physical organs, means there is less room within the physical organ for the healthy light to flow. Contraction, as a result, starts the process of death for the cellular activity of the organ.

It is important to clarify one thing relative to this suggestion. If the scenarios described here were indicative of a "one time affair", meaning that due to a passing but unpleasant incident these fields of light were projected, the effect may indeed be minimal. The physical form of the recipient of these energies may remain unaffected. If, however, either of the following two conditions applies, then the changes to physiology may be more permanent. Firstly, if a person has repeatedly been exposed to similar experiences of the same emotional structure and secondly, if a person's DNA carries forth unhealed potential from his or her ancestral lineage, a greater impact will be evident in the physical form. Hence, of importance at this level is the DNA of your parents, as is also the environment in which consciousness is exposed to Self-reflection. It pays us to remain ever aware that all thoughtforms, especially those that are constantly fed, become real in the Dream. They will seek feeding always and never leave. They become either guide dogs or pet demons. Either way they need to be fed.

Fortunately, by utilizing our fundamental principle that everything is a suggestion or possibility, we may easily arrive at stage one of the solution! Which is to do what? To create language that is powerful in the affirmative mode. Positively affirm the qualities of life and open your self to the Power Before Thought. Allow this Source energy to flood the Dream in which all of your perceived issues of separation and/or disconnection from Source have their foundation. If this sounds too simple, let me offer validation through the story of a telling encounter I had years ago with a great Soul and teacher to me on the path.

THREE DAYS BY BUS, TRAIN AND FOOT...

Many years ago I taught a consciousness training programme in India. Despite the fact that India is the source for much of the material in this arena that has infiltrated western thought, this particular course was one of the very early classes offered publicly by a foreign visitor. Part of the delivery involved a one evening talk that was free. The room was packed to the gills and a ninety-minute sharing evolved into an extended evening of question and answer. All things philosophical and the like were covered. As I endeavoured to close the evening from the front, a significant mass of the crowd swelled forward in a tidal wave of answer seeking. One by one they asked their questions, until finally one older gentleman - who looked like he had seen much of life - stood before me. I would estimate he was in his late sixties to early seventies. He took hold of my hand and spoke. "Please *Swami*, heal my wife. She is sick and dying. I need your blessing," he implored. Needless to say, I was not then nor am I now a Swami, and so his question threw me completely. Yet I looked into his eyes and saw both determination and angst. "I have travelled three days by bus, train and foot for your blessings. Please!" he strained. There was little I could do, since by now he had me by the hand and the heartstrings and would let go of neither. "Just your word is sufficient. Please Swami."

Not knowing what to do, and being some twenty-five years younger at the time, I looked at him, placed my hand on his head and simply said, "So be it." That I felt pretty badly in so doing was a given. But he smiled with joy and left immediately. Enough said, the evening closed and all and sundry went home.

Six months later, back home in Perth, Western Australia, I received a letter postmarked in India. I opened it and read it. It was written in English and was addressed to me as "Swami". It was from this faithful Indian husband who had sought a healing for his wife. He had found one of my sponsors and acquired my address. Then he had asked a friend who wrote a little English to pen a letter for him. What did it say? Simple and concise words. "Thank you for healing my wife. She is now completely cured of her disease and the doctors are amazed." Another few words were added and a signing off with his extended gratitude.

Did I heal his wife? No, not at all. In fact my only role was to act as an instrument for him to channel his own desire, belief and expectancy, across the physical landscape, to his wife. She then, in turn, having the same extent of desire, belief and expectancy, channeled this awareness into a healing. In addition to the powerful lesson in healing this presents to us is what it tells us about consciousness, irrespective of our chosen spiritual path.

There is little or no benefit in slotting this story into a simple category called "faith". Faith has its own baggage and limitations. The Dream is not tethered to the already long existent constructs surrounding faith. To see everything in this light is to limit the Power Before Thought.

There exists within the Dream a higher, grander, and more profound relationship to the Absolute! It is one that lies beyond words, beyond description. It implies connection to this power that is so deep, abiding and potent that it is held as a *yearning*: A yearning that drives one to sacrifice the Dream, in all its aspects, in order to touch this place of great beauty. This is a point of communion that cannot be measured, assessed, or quantified, for it is all embracing, all encompassing, and without limit. It is a potent tool in our quest.

ELIMINATE THE SHADOWS

We now know that the Physical Body makes adaptations to the emotions. Equally so, the Emotional Body is directed from a higher light source, the Mental Body. Once more highlighted for us here is the power of beliefs, attitudes and dispositions in the Dream. Beliefs are experienced as inner world projections and also espoused in language as ideas (architecturally designed within the Dream). They are projected and are either expansive or limiting in their effect. Beliefs have a profound impact on health and well being. A change in beliefs has an equally profound impact. Still higher light bodies, or energetic frequencies, pour through the structures of our consciousness. These are the spiritual aspects of our being. Ultimately, pure health, pure abundance, and pure bliss are all tied to our relationship, as the Observer, to *The Power Before Thought.*

Our quest for expansion forces us to look inward, knowing that anything blocking the free flow of light is creating a shadow inside our Dream. Wherever there are shadows there will be darkness. Wherever there is darkness there will be fear, and wherever there is fear there will always be contraction. Our role is to move beyond contraction and into expansion. As you make this move, it serves you to know that, "Your life is your message and your message is your life." Let us look at the message your life is offering. Is it *your* message, or is it one that you have adopted from some other aspect of your being? If you have adopted it, you have allowed yourself to play a part in another's Dream.

The Power Before Thought This highlights the issue of your personal *will*. If you have adopted your message from another within the Dream, you have willed yourself, and as a result projected yourself, into playing a role that is not of Truth to your Self. If this is done, by an act of deferring your will to that of another player in the field of the Dream, your message will not be that of your own. You will be surrendering your potential to experience the fullness of all that creation has to offer.

Ultimately, however, in order to escape the gravitational field of the lower Dream, your will, associated with the Self, must align itself with the driving force of the *Will* that is integral to the Power Before Thought. If your (Self) directs your will to harmonize all aspects of your being towards the Greater Good, then all aspects will transform in the name of the Greater Good. You will become a portal for the free flow of the Power of which we speak. To work with this alignment of the lesser will with the Greater Will it benefits us to consider how our thoughts, words and deeds are intricately associated with the illusion that time is real. Past hurts bring forth future woes. Future fears eliminate current joy. The nexus is so deeply ingrained in our Dream that without a consideration of the significance of time, there is a noose around us that we may indeed have difficulty transcending.

Time

"As if you could kill time without injuring eternity."
Henry David Thoreau

Most people see the concept of time as pretty straightforward. Time is seen to be linear in nature. It is a quantifiable commodity and measurable in units that delineate our existence into past, present and future. These units are most commonly known as seconds, minutes, hours, days, weeks, months, years, decades, centuries and, of course, millennium. Humanity measures its existence against these units and utilizes clocks to create the illusion of the rigidity and solidity of events. Clocks, in turn, further solidify the classical Newtonian position of a material world in which the universe is a machine; a universe in which mastery of the world must be undertaken in order to create desirable outcomes.

Within the structure of these Newtonian laws, mind and matter are seen as separate and do not interact. Matter itself is subject to the laws while mind, being non-physical, is separate from these laws. In context of this, we have a series of "markers" or "benchmarks" against which we measure our existence and particular accomplishments. Finances, relationships, health, education, the history of humanity, wisdom, and many subsets within these, are all regarded as being intimately related to time. This would be fine except for one thing...Time is an illusion - a suggestion, just like everything else!

THE OCEAN

Mystics of nearly every ancient tradition regarded time as somewhat akin to an ocean through which we swim. We live within an ocean of time. It is all around us and yet it passes through us at every level of our Being. We are washed by the tides of time in many different directions. Our body ages with time yet our Spirit is timeless. There is part of us that is in no way influenced by time nor subject to its unfolding. To the ancients (and modern day mystics including quantum physicists), time is cyclical and yet expansively repetitive. In like manner to the solar cycles, the lunar cycles, digestive cycles, and so forth, the whole universe is cyclical and replete with repetitive states. These repetitive states ebb and flow in a grand evolutionary scheme that no human mind can truly grasp.

There is an interconnectivity across these cycles where an earlier equivalent of the same cycle comes forth but brings with it new blossoms of possibility. Yet we must not think of this as a cycle of set time, such as 5,000 years, in which we all simply reincarnate to do the same thing again and again. No, rather, cyclical time is deeper and more profound. From the quantum perspective there is no certainty at all. Everything is a possibility, and all possibilities truly do exist at some level within the infinite limitless expanse of the Dream. One of these possibilities, expanding beyond quantum fields of realization, is that which lies outside of creation. That which lies outside can be considered to be the Dreamer. The Dreamer is the One that conceives of time and space and all the illusionary possibilities that propagate the deeper illusion of the unreality we call the Dream.

VEHICLES OF CONSCIOUSNESS

In one of my classes, I employ a simple model and a useful analogy to convey an idea of how we interact with time. Follow this analogy with me, for it will help you understand that which follows. Consider that there are a number of ways you could travel from New York to London. One is by air, boarding an aircraft in New York and arriving seven hours later in Heathrow. A second is by ocean voyage, travelling on a liner from the port of New York and arriving in Southampton six days later. A third, perhaps courtesy of the US government, is by travel on a submarine, departing from a base somewhere near New York and arriving, once again, in Southampton. Here we have three different vehicles all transporting the one unit of consciousness - you, or the Intelligence that you are - across the physical space between two locations on planet Earth.

These vehicles of travel can be compared to what we call the *Vehicles of Consciousness of our Being.* The Vehicles of Consciousness are thoughtforms created within the Dream to facilitate the transfer of awareness - or perceptive experiences - from one locale (time and space) to another. Each operates most efficiently in its own, best-suited medium and not in an alternate, unsuited medium. This is easy to understand if one imagines how placing a submarine at the end of a runway at JFK airport, or placing a Boeing 747 at the docks in New York, would accomplish little and get us nowhere fast. If we can see how these distinct physical vehicles of transportation serve their function best in their own mediums and for differing functions of travel, we can likewise perceive how we, as a multi-faceted Being, would have physical and non-physical vehicles of "transportation" that assist us to navigate differing dimensions of the Dream.

We, as Being, have in this model four thoughtform vehicles that exist within the Dream through which we experience time and space, or rather time/space. Firstly, we have the *Physical Body*, through which we experience *linear* time and space. Secondly, we have the vehicle of the *Soul*, through which we have the experience of time as *a day of 1000 years*. Thirdly, we have the vehicle of *Spirit*, through which time is experienced as an *eternity*. Our fourth vehicle, our *Divine Spark*, is the vehicle through which we experience *timelessness*. Remember, all of this is a suggestion. All is a model to help us understand our unreal nature of being Human. If we can understand how to master these vehicles, we can rapidly move through and beyond the need for them.

In effect, we are saying that there are three primary Vehicles of Consciousness through which we experience time. Note that only one operates through time/space as we know it, and that is where the physical vehicle resides. Each of the other Vehicles of Consciousness displays a different manner of operating inside the Dream. Hence, associated with each of these vehicles, inside the Dream, are a very specific series of correspondences, as listed below. Let's look at them now.

Dimension	Vehicle	Time	Expression
Emanation	Divine Spark	Timelessness	Theos
Creation	Spirit	Eternity	Logos
Formation	Soul	Day of 1,000 Years	Mythos
Action	Physical Body	Linear Time	Ethos

These particular understandings have their foundation in mystery teachings from Western Tradition. While profound realizations can be gleaned from deep study of Tradition, I ask you to resist a heavy thought process and just dance with me for a moment. This, like everything else, is merely a suggestion. A statement of possibility. It is not fixed, rigid, or absolute. It is a thoughtform to help explain what is happening in your life. Merely tapping on the gate to these suggestions will offer us exactly what we require for now.

The above table shows the relationship of time to the vehicle best suited to carry our Observer aspect throughout specific experiences in the Dream. Hence we have the level of the Dream that we are engaging tied very specifically to the vehicle and an experience of time. How the Observer experiences the dimension of time is all about how it expresses itself inside the Dream. These are the fields that help us understand and rise above the limitations encoded within the Mass Cultural Hypnosis of the lesser Dream. When you master these understandings The Power Before Thought will unleash itself into the Dream that you are evolving through.

MANAGING OUR RIDE

Ethos

At any single moment in time, as an Observer, all four aspects of our Being are conscious. The awareness of our total Being, however, is primarily locked into one significant point of focus. This point of focus becomes what we create, or rather collapse into, as reality. Hence, when we believe with absolute conviction that we are physical beings, accept the images of the world at large, and justify our present by referencing our past, we are creating through a *linear-time locked Dream.* Our Physical Body is guided within the Dream by a code of ethics, either our own or those adopted from cultural sources such as religious institutions, political allegiances, or other philosophical movements. We live within the field of this *Ethos* and do so with both its blessings *and* limitations.

Mythos

We gain further support for this state of rigidly and repetitive behavior through our Soul. The Soul, in the above model, is deeply involved in the field of the myth. It is working with what is called *Mythos.* Mythos comprises the historical thoughtforms that form our current cultural and more expansive reality spanning time and space. We refer to time here as representing *"a day of 1000 years".* In this teaching the Soul exists in a much broader context of time. It is through this portal of time that the tuning fork of our inner Being brings forth greater potentials from within the life experience of our Being. For through this portal the Soul resonates either with physically liberating realizations, or with physically debilitating limitations from concurrently existing parallel (past and future) lives. The past life understandings have their foundation here. People who live out of a higher myth driven reality tend to cross time/space with greater ease, and experience a different reality, than those tied to the ethics of linear time/space alone. Note: the Soul is not tied to a clock!

Logos

Equally important to our understanding is our knowing that, at all moments in time, another active part of our spiritual intelligence is working. This part is functioning in an even higher field of awareness that we call *Logos*. Logos is a Greek word that, in layman's terms, means "the order and pattern of things and how they are related to the whole." The key here is to comprehend that the field of the Spirit, and all of its sub-vehicles, is one of high reason, intellectual perception, and creative use of ratio and proportions to perceive relationships in a whole. The Spirit provides the access point and vehicle within the Dream through which sacred geometric form and function are installed and activated. An example of this is your direct experience of the Logos through the sacred structures of the codes that underlie your physical existence - namely, your DNA.

This seems like a good moment to remind you that your DNA is not set in stone, unchanging or definitive at birth. It can be altered by conscious awareness. The Observer, as an expression of the Power Before Thought, is the consciousness that can redirect, or rather, *will* the changes of which we speak. The first point of shift becomes the Spirit. If we are dumbed down to the existence of this vehicle, then we are subservient to the lower vehicles. The lower vehicles have an extensive array of thoughtforms to support our staying there. Hence myths and ethics abound as our limiting,

48

self-separating aspects of Being.

The Logos shows its presence on a larger scale through the order that appears out of the field of apparent chaos. This apparent random chaos yields magnificent beauty in the Dream. At a core level it is the dimension in which all codes of all possible creative endeavors are held in suspension. All morphic fields gather their codes for manifestation into ideas at this level of the Dream. At the very highest level of Spirit, inside the Dream, within the Logos, there are streams of order, colour and patterning that create thoughtforms which we perceive as gods and goddesses. Those who touch this level of perception are able to provide deep and wise discourse upon the higher levels of the Dream. These wise ones are sages, or seers of the ages.

Time, here in Logos, is regarded as an *eternity*. Actually one or more eternities, for there is not just one eternity. This is a very creative point within the Dream. Creation is tied to harmony, and harmony is patterned in both nature and the nature of our Being. All that is less than harmony in thought, word or deed is what lies at the base of discontent in our unreal reality. When you restore harmony to all aspects of the Dream, your life will automatically follow suit. It is really not that hard...as we shall ultimately discover.

Theos

When we pierce the level of Spirit and align with higher levels of perception, we are in communion with the highest vehicle of which we are aware. Above and beyond this there is no known vehicle, and for us to define one would be counter-productive. This level is what is called the *Divine Spark*. This Light is beyond thoughtform and expresses itself through the field of *Theos*. Theos is not the Source but is of the Source. Humanity has taken this word Theos and its many derivatives, as well as other ancient terms, and lumped them all together to form the concept, or thoughtform, of "God". A lot of our problems inside the Dream come from this gross generalization.

Theos, for our purposes, implies that our timeless link into the Dream has its core anchor in something that is both within and beyond the Dream - both immanent and transcendent. This core is a Divine Spark of the Source itself (by whatever name one chooses to assign to Source). This level of the Dream is that of *Emanation*, or that which pours forth from the Power Before Thought and streams into Creation, enthusing the Logos with Light to activate the sacred codes. Here we are touching the Dreamer and His/Her Dream directly.

Each of these vehicles of consciousness can be considered as having many different hues and colours. The Soul, for instance, has infinite Soul aspects, some of which are anchored in one experience, and others of which are Light Years away. The same can be said for the Spirit and for the Divine Spark. Let us, therefore, not become tied up in analysis, for this will merely circumvent our expansion.

BENDING THE MIND

To bend the mind a bit more just for fun, and to glimpse the infinite magnitude of the concept of "time", we need only to add the teachings of ancient Indian Tradition to those of Western Mystery School Tradition. Time, in India, is known as *Kala*. It is expansive and covers everything from a *Truti*, which is approximately 0.031 microsecond (a microsecond being one millionth of a second), through to what is known as a *Maha Kalpa*. A Maha Kalpa is 311 trillion years, wherein a year is prescribed to be 365 days. While a brief study of Vedic teachings will reveal all of the complexity involved in moving from a Truti through to a Maha Kalpa, we'll skip that part. Think of this understanding of time from the Vedas and you will see how our current clock-driven unreality leaves a lot to be desired. Why? Because these ancients knew that infinite possibilities existed in a *moment*, which they deemed as being measurable, by human consciousness, as only 0.031 microseconds.

The ancients also knew that Human expansiveness was

not related to the unreal dream of a calendar created by a being who wished humanity to follow a physical Dream rather than a spiritual Dream. Remember, there have been numerous calendars, all drawn from sacred geometric cycles in the Logos, expressed through the myth by gods and goddesses, and manifested in the unreal Dream by way of clocks and timepieces. Humanity operates, worldwide, according to the Gregorian calendar, and we have done so since 1582. This calendar has its origins in the Christian faith and has since become the worldwide timepiece for economic and financial dealings and, in the larger scale, the monitoring of the worldwide evolution of our species. It was imposed upon humanity by an order! The myth changed, and so did the ethics that flowed from this myth. In our current unreal Dream, there are cycles that are not able to be pre-determined, and they operate within the artificial calendar of the markets. Here we see the rise and fall of stock markets, the life cycle of epidemics, and the endless list of cyclical aspects of the Dream.

There have been many other calendars, some of which still operate in subdivisions of human existence across the planet: the Babylonian, Chinese, Muslim, Jewish, Egyptian, Coptic, Roman, Julian, Japanese, Hindu, and more. There is the Maya calendar, which has asked us to look into the heavens and grasp understanding of the Dream and the unreality of our limited concept of self. If time is an illusion, then that which measures the illusion, upon which we place so much faith and regulate our short lives, must also be – an illusion. It is one that exists at the very lowest end of creation when it is used to manipulate the Mass Cultural Hypnosis.

Our interest here is to know how these suggestions, and the keys to Self knowledge they offer, assist us in our lives and our understanding of the Dream. When we bring together some of the "loopholes" that the Dream has presented to us, we begin to make sense of how we can work to create abundance, love, light, and joy in this magnificent universe. Not only for ourselves, but also for all of creation. Let us continue our exploration and depth of insight, and let us reach our goal, for everything in creation has its origin there, in The Power Before Thought.

Before Time Began

"A single ray of light from a distant star falling upon the eye of a tyrant in bygone times may have altered the course of his life, may have changed the destiny of nations, may have transformed the surface of the globe, so intricate, so inconceivably complex are the processes in Nature."
Nikola Tesla

Our last chapter revealed merely a glimpse of the magnitude of the human experience relative to time. In context of this glimpse, it serves us to consider a few famous words from Western Tradition. The first words of the *Bible's Book of Genesis* read, *"In the beginning was the word…"* (Again, I ask you to note that I refer to the Bible rather than the sacred text of another Tradition to illustrate a point using a familiar reference for many Western readers.) Within this phrase, "the beginning" represents a benchmark. It marks the delineation between something that already exists and something just beginning. In biblical context, it indicates the beginning of Creation; Creation being the point at which *time* (at the level of our traditional comprehension of the concept) begins. It implies also that there was *something* which came before Creation, and that which was before pertains to the creative Source or Dreamer (in the indigenous model of the Dream). It is the inception point for the manifestation of the Dream. There is an implied Power behind the revelation of the beginning of time. *Time is a thought projected by this Power.*

As a physical phenomenon viewed through the eyes of our physical being, this Creation point can be seen to have occurred Light Years in the past - in time and space - as the very first Creation of the Universe and Earth. Yet perceived through our Being as the Divine Spark, we understand this point to be a constant, never dying moment of the here and now. This understanding is vital to our exploration. Because we exist at all levels in all dimensions, including that level beyond Creation, then we, as Divine Spark, in a pre-Dream state, collectively existed and still exist before time began. This collective existence *before* time began is actually somewhat greater than it sounds. *It implies that we are all One, yet simultaneously infinite possibilities of the One that are, as of yet, to become sentient and create within the Matrix of Light - that which is the Dream.*

Light Years do not even come close to exploring the infinite nature of our Being, but they do reveal something significant. No matter how far away in time and space the imprints of our thoughtforms appear to have first been formed, at whatever end of the spectrum of the Universe, *they are still now, and always have been, sentient and active in a "post"- Divine Spark sense, which is the here and now.*

ALL POTENTIAL IS POSSIBLE RIGHT NOW!

Because we exist *within, through* and *before* time began, we have within us the ultimate capacity to re-engineer the experience of our currently perceived reality. To BE what we came here to BE. Yet we are not limited to the currently perceived reality. *We also have the capacity to change the perspective of reality on all levels - past, present and future! In other words, we can Dream our way back to the Dreamer.* This is about our beingness not our humanness.

Our creation, and all that we perceive within it, is in the hands of the Divine Spark. The Divine Spark is an aspect of the Divine Self, and the Divine Self is an aspect of the One. If we want to change the world we live in, we must transcend our illusionary perception of time and space. Reality inside the Dream is a construct of light. Light informs our experience. To change reality we must *The Power Before* change our relationship to light. Put another way, we must vibrate *Thought* differently to that which we have been vibrating. Put yet another way, we must BE different. This is about being a *Human Being*, one who is outside the constraints of time and space as we know it.

PLAYING WITH LIGHT

Consider the following. Light, as we understand it, travels at 186,000 miles per second. Based on this calculation, light from our Sun, which is 93 million miles away, takes just over eight minutes to reach us here on Earth. A Light Year is the distance that light travels in one year of 365 days. A Light Year is calculated in the obvious manner of 60 seconds by 60 minutes by 24 hours by 365 days. The result is that light will travel 5,865,696,000,000 miles in one Light Year.

To know and experience our reality at the point before the Dream began, all we would need to do, theoretically, is to travel back through space at the speed of light to the point at which the beginning of our Maha Kalpa began. Based on this accepted model of calculation, our travel would take 311.04 trillion years. (In the American measurement system, a trillion is a million million, but in Indian measurement, based in the British Imperial system, a trillion is even greater, tallying as one million million million.) Thus the latter model tells us it would take us 53,026,955.369 years to travel at the speed of light back to Source. In "American" years, it would take a lot less, but still a whacking 53,026 years - non-stop of course - to get there. We would, therefore, need to travel just a little bit faster to get there *before* time began.

To arrive before time began, however, would present us with a challenge (assuming the rest of this would be a piece of cake!). It

54

is perhaps more a philosophical challenge than anything else, but still a consideration. If we were set on arriving before time began then we, along with time, would not have been dreamed into existence. Hence travelling back this way would either age us in a sincerely boring manner or delete us from existence upon arrival at the point of origin. Neither of these are desirable outcomes. All of this assumes, of course, that there was not another Maha Kalpa that was accessible just prior to the collapse of the current one we are travelling through. If that were the case we could continue this journey, ad infinitum, until we exhausted all possibilities, lost all individuality, and dissolved into the light. Either way, what we know is that such travel is physically not within the reach of any of us. I would posit this journey would also be out of reach for any alien life force that might inhabit our cosmos as well, for they too would also be operating inside the field of the Dream. The Dream is a construct of Maya and governed by the rules of Maya.

FASTER THAN THE SPEED OF LIGHT

There is another way however, to travel. Another way to reach "possible" dreams. When Einstein told us that nothing travels faster than the speed of light, what he was really saying was that there was nothing *known* that was measurable as travelling faster than the speed of light. He was correct, yet there *is* something faster than the speed of light that is *not measurable*, for it exists outside the paradigm of our constructs of mind. *It is the Light behind the light that is the Thought of Being.* The thought to *become* is that which precedes the Dream. Between each moment, behind every breath, prior to, during and after each thought, there are infinite possible virgin Trutis, or .030 microseconds units, of potential untapped thought. *These thoughts are free of structure, untapped and ready to be breathed into reality across the spectrum of creation.*

Dissolving The Thought Of Consciousness

*"You may say I'm a dreamer, but I'm not the only one.
I hope someday you'll join us. And the world will live as one."*
John Lennon

Travel implies crossing time and space. We can delete reference to that concept since we are not here engaged in travel. We are engaged in *Being*. As a Human Being we are active in all of our vehicles, in time/space, without hindrance. We are rising above the limitations of these fields of expression and focusing on a deeper reality. Hence we do not need to travel back to the point of Creation, we simply need to be ONE with that point of Creation - which we already are and always have been.

Becoming one with that point also makes us one with all that exists in the field, or matrix, of the entire Dream. To have become aware of this point where the Dream begins is to have a vista, and acute awareness, of the power and potency of the design or Logos of the Dream. That means we are looking into the matrix from before the Dream began, and we can see how the infinite parts of our multiple selves, (past lives, future selves, current other selves – 7 billion alone on Earth right now in human form) have created thoughtforms inside the Dream. We can also see how some of these are responsible for uplifting creation, and how others are responsible for holding it back from the Greater Good. All perfect, of course.

The power of these thoughtforms is such that they exist, in and of themselves, as separate entities inside the Dream. Each thoughtform has its own sentient existence. Understanding the structures of thought, their potency, mode of operation, and the consequences of NOT being master of them, is where we now head. In doing so we must cross the boundary of the time/space Dream to observe, completely, through the consciousness of the Divine Spark monitoring the Logos in its creative informing of the unfolding Dream. Then we must direct our awareness into the Mythos, looking at the influence of the mass hypnosis of the myth that drives creation. Finally, as the Observer, we direct our awareness into how it has driven our beingness into wonder and awe, or instead into limitation and separation.

Therefore, in essence, we will travel back to the point of Creation, which we have just explored, to completely re-engineer the constructs of our reality. Through the Power Before Thought, we will employ our beingness for the Greater Good. In so doing, we will also understand how and why we appear to have experiences throughout our lives that don't seem to be our own. We are tapping into the matrix of limitless thoughtforms of the no time/space Dream through varying aspects of our Self, through use of our Vehicles of Consciousness, and having multi-faceted experiences of life all at once. Not bad! You are a limitless, multi-dimensional Being existing with the capacity to have power, awareness and presence in all existence without limit. All for the Greater Good.

BACK TO THE FUTURE

How does one, therefore, experience the point of Creation? Through thought, of course! What type of thought? Those extremely potent, high level thoughts resident within the Dream that rise up above the lower Maya and into the higher reaches of love. It may appear here and now to be a time and space oriented process, but it is one that eventually leads us to Self-realization and is well worth the effort! It is possible because we have *Self Reflective Consciousness* - that which drives us to "get to know" our beingness. Can this Self knowing happen instantaneously? Perhaps. Can it take time in a linear sense? Also, perhaps. It does not, however, have to take 53,000 years to experience, unless we choose this option. Why? Because the mind, when unfettered by the illusion and detached from the drag of lower vibrational energies within the Dream, can instantly perceive the Source Point and both feel and know the power of detachment, dissolution of lower self and mergence into that which exists before thought.

Exciting, right! Tapping an infinite power source and support for your personal creative evolution, and that of humanity within the Dream, through our interconnectedness - all by your Self! Let us now move into the realm of how this works.

WHAT YOU SEE IS WHAT YOU GET

All perceptions of image, feeling, emotion, intuition and other modalities - all of what we experience through the Dream - are, first and foremost, structures of thought. These perceptions are architecturally engineered inside the consciousness of one or more individuals and then projected within the higher realms of vibration into manifestation. *Images we perceive in the physical world are manifestations of the captured imprints from Spirit.* They contain the "codex", if you will, or Logos imprint, of a formula of light and sound made manifest. Physical images are structures of thought - encapsulating light - transferred dimensionally into our Self Reflective Consciousness: Formless light into formulae into form into function.

A short anecdote will illuminate how this process unfolds in the Dream. As I have previously stated, I have worked with clients in a healing modality for many years. I become the instrument of Self-reflection for their consciousness. On one particular occasion I was shown, in Spirit, a situation that had developed in the current life incarnation of a client. I was then shown a time frame during which the situation was revealed to have manifested. As our session evolved I was shown parallel universe implications of the situation. It involved aspects of other Souls and other entities across time and space. The situation, involving the overall well being of the Soul concerned, was shown to be associated with a series of specific images and symbols. These images and symbols were imprinted as specific physical photographs that had been in the person's possession in the past. The photographic images held power. They encapsulated an energetic imprint within the matrix of time and space.

The client had worked with many, many images, through the medium of photography. This had played a significant part in his life journey. These photographs were associated with his work, and pertained to a time frame many years prior, in this lifetime, during which he developed a series of challenges. These challenges were the basis of his real time, here and now, healing, even though they entered his life many years before. These images, stored as photographs, were, as was later revealed, Soul-destroying images. They were taken for a major publication (for presentation in printed media) and many displayed horrific scenes of war. That which was shown to me in Spirit was simple. The client had, through interaction with these photographs, taken on a direct Soul link to the energetic imprint in the Dream of those who were undergoing the suffering. These direct links were then impacting upon his Soul.

These images portrayed other Souls - Souls who were suffering. The photos were images that stored energetic moments in time/space. Since all time/space is here and now, these photos brought the despair of the Souls concerned into the real-time

Dream experience of my client. They had a strong and potent impact upon his Mythos, a lot of which we all keep hidden and unconscious. As we shared earlier, when this part of our Being is out of balance, all else follows suit. We fall out of harmony, and in so doing we lose the integrity of our Being. Integrity being the wholeness, or completeness of our total Self. To integrate or make ONE is the ultimate purpose of all healing. *These images, on paper, encoded energetic disruptions in that unified field and called upon the Soul carrying those imprints to take action to resolve the pain. It is only when action is taken that the healing begins. It begins not just for the client/Soul, but also for all aspects of all Souls. I.e. The Greater Good.*

It is vital to our journey that we truly grasp the significance of this person's experience. For we all share in this, as well as in experiences individual to each of us. As highly charged images - just like highly active "dogs" they follow us throughout our lives. Again, let us use an example to illustrate how this suggestion works in every day life, for it reveals so much of what might seem inexplicable in our daily experience. Imagine that you are looking at a scene filled with beautiful roses, fauna, and blue skies. Joy-filled children are frolicking and a cricket match is being played in the background. The impact of these images upon your Being might be one of relative peace, but overall the impact is neutral. There is no negative impact upon you. Now, imagine that you are observing images on TV of a horrific war scene. Your Soul is impacted by these images. Initially it would appear that you experience a feeling of horror, perhaps shock, or dread upon seeing the display of what one human can do to another. The feelings may last a few minutes, perhaps hours or even days, but eventually they would appear to drift away. Yet this is not so, and knowledge of this is a major clue to understanding how the Dream really works.

These images of war have linked your higher Soul beingness to the Soul aspects of your own Being that were undergoing the experience. *There is a direct, quantum, non-specific, non-linear, causal relationship between "you" and "them" established across time and space.* All images have impact, as do all sounds and all thoughts. The fact that we do not receive the impact of all sounds and thoughts does not negate the fact that we do experience many that have not originated from ourselves directly. This simply reveals further how we create the Dream. We possess the mechanism to filter out, from the infinite possibilities we encounter, those primary thoughtforms and images upon which we choose to focus and through which we choose to act. *We "collapse into being" what our intent desires us to, through our individual will.*

You are One with all aspects of the Dream. Every thought, word and deed of every being has an impact upon your Dream. How you reconcile this within yourself determines how you live out your life path. It establishes the difference between living in service to your life's fullest purpose or surrendering to the fate of a culturally hypnotized mass. You are far greater than anything you can observe, so why surrender to the lesser Dream? Can you do something about this? Can you break free of the lesser Dream into a greater Dream and beyond the Dream in a productive and positive manner? Yes!

YOU, THE CREATOR

Remember, time is at your fingertips! You are greater than time as long as you do not believe yourself to be your Physical, Emotional or Mental Body. If you fall into this trap, however, you are subject once more to time and it will have its way with you. The timeless Observer, the part of you that is - even before the Divine Spark, and which is aligned to the Source of all that is - has the capacity to change your experience of time/space. You can clear the energetic imprint of any time/space experience and in so doing clear it's impact on your Soul. Put another way, *you can travel back in time to the point before the event occurred in linear time and you can dismiss the authority of the images seen and their recorded impact upon you.* You exist before these codings of light came into being. If you do not like them then you can change them at Source. You also change their impact upon the DNA and what may be physically passed forth to other generations.

You might be asking yourself, "If this is truly possible, why don't we all do this every minute of every day?" The reason so many choose not to do this is twofold. Firstly, there is a culturally accepted belief that this is not possible, mainly due to the fact that dominant classical physics still informs society on its norms. Secondly, and of even greater significance, is the human's deep-seated spiritual fear of self-annihilation. In other words, we fear the depths to which we might have to delve into ourselves to truly heal and release all of these imprints of limitation. Given our current understanding of ourselves as Human Beings and the belief that we live in an age of material dominance, it is best to take this process of cleaning out step by step. As we address and move from lesser issues to deeper ones, we gradually detach from the drag of the lower vibratory fields. It is the move from self to the Self; from personal good to Greater Good. This is what the mystics call the *Great Work*, or the conscious evolution of God. In other words, God becomes God becomes God becomes God, ad infinitum, until that which can no longer be determined actually is. We then are ONE with that which we cannot define.

HEY, WHAT ABOUT MY KARMA?

You might be tempted to say also, "This is all well and good for linear time, since we can track back along a frame of reference in our present lifetime, but how about past and future lives? How do we deal with them without a frame of reference?" Here the whole issue of karma and cause-effect raises its head. Yet we know that karma is a suggestion inside the Dream. It is not an absolute. We, at our highest level inside the Dream, created this law to help us rise above it! Karma is a code within the Logos. Above the code is a higher Truth. Aspiring to be consciously Self-reflective enables us to rise above the lower trappings of these karmic impressions.

What does this mean? It means that we don't have to worry about our past lives! We don't have to try to remember them,

The Power Before
Thought

regress to them, or anything of that sort. We merely have to be in the "present". Then the "past" and "future", all of which is non-determined, will fall in line. Because deep within the time/space warp, past and future lives exist here and now. Images from thirty years ago are an imprint of sound and light - in time and space - that we can consciously experience here and now. What about an image that is 3000 years old? It is, likewise, a series of thoughtforms impregnated as light that you can feel, sense and experience within the collapsed possibility of the Dream that we call *"this dimension"*. How does it work? Upon viewing the images, we activate the energy within the formula that is this image inside the Dream, and then we experience a Soul reaction.

If you truly want to heal this world, and all of your life, then you must have the courage to look deeply into all of Creation and bring it forth into your own Self, absorb all the energy of each aspect, and release it back - as purified light - to Source. This is the ultimate act of sacrifice, and it brings the lower self into conflict with the higher Self. It is the battle between the ego and the Divine. It is best, therefore, that we have good reason to work with this transformative creative process, for then we will do our work with greater conviction and determination. A look at how we embrace and work with this worthy effort, to reach into the Power Before Thought and create a greater Dream for ourselves and humanity, requires that we search deeply for the keys held in the Dream. To do this we return to where we began on our journey together.

111

Walking In The Dream

Qualities Of Thought

"Never limit yourself because of others' limited imagination;
never limit others because of your own limited imagination."
Mae Jemison, First African American Astronaut

Knowing how to enact the infinite potential for change and
create a greater Dream requires that we continue our exploration
and understanding of how we, as creators in the Dream, have
constructed reality. In earlier chapters we touched upon the
manner in which this construction relates to myth, both cultural
and personal. We return here to the power of myth to strengthen
the fabric of our understanding.

Few would question the notion that western societies create
reality in a different manner than that employed by indigenous
peoples. All methods have merit, but I propose that we draw
upon the wisdom of indigenous peoples to provide insight
into principles most key to the creation process we seek to
engage. Indigenous peoples around the world live outside the
common matrix of thought that is promulgated and fertilized
by contemporary society. Indigenous peoples have shamanic
cultures that enable them, when they are trained in their

mythology, to cross time and space and enter into alternate realities.

These realities are not commonly understood by much of the somewhat sanitized segments of our 21st century information society. They do, however, offer us many gifts through maintaining their presence in the "modern" world. One unique and priceless gift is the window of clarity they open for us as we view the impact and potency of thought on our planet. Through understanding the nature of their realities we see clearly the tremendous power of thought and also how, through use of this powerful faculty of human consciousness, we may be unwittingly and collectively manipulated by lower levels of thought projection generated within society and fostered by a desire for control. Then we are able to clearly see also that we have the power to change - through realization of that which we have unwittingly surrendered to.

The Dream of which we have spoken may be a new concept for non-indigenous peoples, but for the aboriginal peoples of the world it provides the fabric of their myth - a very powerful fabric. Each myth has its own vibrational potency. Each is rich with its own symbols, colours, sounds, and feelings. An individual myth is generally found to be subservient to a family myth, and that myth in turn becomes subservient to tribal, community, racial, gender and nation state myths. Nevertheless, all myth has power. The real issue is, however, not the fact that myths actually exist, but rather the degree to which humanity today has surrendered power unto the mass myth of our times. This mass myth is structured and directed by powerful vibrational tools, the end result of which is a surrender of individual consciousness unto what can sometimes be regarded as a mindless hypnotic reality.

An example at this juncture will be helpful to us as we peel the layers of understanding to reach the deep core truth of how thought, in all its manifest forms, influences each aspect of each Soul across time and space. Thought, the essence of our consciousness, may be directed in many different pathways. There are three primary channels. If we are not consciously working with each of these to uplift creation then we are likely allowing their power to be wasted, hence wasting our lives in the process. Or, we may, unwittingly, be allowing for their use in maintaining lower vibratory levels of existence. These powerful channels are known as *Thought Projection, Thought Linkage* and *Thought Radiance.*

THOUGHT PROJECTION

Projection, as you can imagine, is a time/space experience. It works in the realm of lower vibration and implies, by its very nature, that individual and separate units of consciousness exist in the Dream. Hence, one can project from one unit, or Soul, to another. These thoughtform projections are shaped by the influences currently playing out in our Souls. Disturbances such as fear, anger, and resentment take shape according to the energy they are fed. We then project outward - from our inner Being to a part of our Dream - a thought, shaped by influences that will impact the illusionary separate entity.

THOUGHT LINKAGE

Thought Linkage is a subset of Thought Projection and operates in the field of separation. For analogy purposes it can be likened to hypertext links on a webpage. Whereby, if you scroll your cursor over a word, embedded within the word is a link to another page. Only by clicking that word, activating the link, and going to the linked page, will the impact of the link be revealed. (i.e. Free Dinner for Two!). Here, we can see clearly the import of having the link and the projection acting together. The link is a hidden key that leads to the unlocking of images that carry a new message.

THOUGHT RADIANCE

Thought Radiance also operates within the field of the Dream, yet it does not imply separation. Thought Radiance simply is, and all who engage the radiance experience the richness of the energy.

Let us explore an example.

Imagine with me the following scenario. An image of the current US president will bring up a predictable variety of responses from most people to whom it is shown - in the world of the Mass Cultural Hypnosis. The photo is a thoughtform well established in the Mass Cultural Hypnosis of our world. Amongst American citizens, and throughout the world, the mention of his name, sound of his voice, or sight of his image will generate feelings *(Thought Linkage)* of respect, disdain, love, hate, excitement or a range of other feelings, strong or mild. The reasons for the responses are many, and they can be explained away by any number of disciplines such as psychology, psychiatry, or even religious and new age techniques. It may well be that we grew up persuaded to one political allegiance or another, hence our initial response. It may be that we have a dislike of men, do not trust people in authority, or, conversely, have enormous trust that such authority figures are there to protect and save us. Issues that are culturally engendered such as race, age, and appearance all play their part.

Many are the reasons and each one has its origin deep inside our Being. To understand why we have these responses is, for many, a profound study and science. Unravel the complex human mind! The key for us to note here is that the techniques and methods used by most, if not all, disciplines, including psychiatry and psychology, have their origin in the deep esoteric Mystery Schools' understanding of consciousness. When the Renaissance arrived and we became more enraptured with classical physics and the Newtonian approach to life, we culturally shifted from the inner school wisdom to outer world clinical dissecting of the personae and the Soul. This can provide insights, but rarely does it supply long term resolutions to the overriding issues at stake. The issues of the perception of an individual, event or circumstance in one's life have their origin outside the worldview of the culturally accepted myth, AKA the lower Dream.

Now, imagine that we present the image of our President to a group of indigenous individuals, such as Aboriginal Australians. *Thought Projection* here is simply a showing of the image. Having never been exposed to our cultural hypnosis, they have a *The Power Before* decidedly different experience when looking at the image. There *Thought* is no frame of reference for their engagement with the image at the *physical level*. There is no *Thought Linkage* that is activated. They *know* at the Universal level, yet have no conscious engagement at the physical, emotional or mental levels. It might as well be an image of a stranger they met during walkabout in the desert. As such, there arises no deep and abiding feeling, for no power is given over to the image. The Linkage must have the power of the projection behind it in order to generate an energetic reaction, and the consequent results. Despite the existence of a Soul interaction between the two, due to the photographic imprint in the matrix of creation (recall my client viewing the war scenes), in this scenario there is no direct power conveyed to the Aboriginal viewer. They are linked at a deeper level, but it is not activated. This is a key point. *A connection is made, yet no thoughtform energy has moved from source A to source B.*

What exists in this instance is merely an observation by one Soul part of another. The image is a photo of a man, there is no personae activation within the Soul aspect of the observer, for there is no identification with the image and the image alone holds no intrinsic power of *Radiation. To hold the power of Radiation, the Soul concerned (President) must have a unique awareness of SELF, which takes place during Self-realization.* Analogous to this, most of us, if shown an image of a revered piece of Aboriginal rock art, would have a similar, indifferent response. We would interpret it as we see fit and probably use some of the subconscious references within our state of being to help us make sense of what we experience.

There is another level of meaning to consider within this example. What has transpired illustrates at a mundane level how the principle of Thought Projection works within creation. When we have a familiar construct of thoughtforms in which we bathe, we will tap into that pool of constructs upon seeing the images we recognize, and this will elicit from our Emotional or Mental Body a predictable result. Visual recognition is but a frequency of response from one and all. The indigenous Soul may have many different levels of recognition. This may be due to the nature of thought. We respond differently to sunlight than to the light which pours forth from a flashlight.

RADIANCE IS YOUR NATURE

Radiant thoughts at the lower dimensional level of humanity's beingness are radiations of energy, inside a grander spectrum of the Dream. They do not find themselves limited to time and space. Hence an image that radiates light, love and joy, yet is one of a particular cultural source (e.g. a Buddha), may in itself generate the same energetic response inside a Soul who lives within another culture (e.g. a Christian). The image simply acts as a portal to link into an energetic imprint in the matrix of creation.

We can use another photographic example to illustrate better the power of Thought Radiation in the Dream. Imagine along with me once more. Let us take a photograph of a Christian ascetic who is deeply meditating on the inner relationship he has with Jesus, which creates within this ascetic an aura of innocent love and light. This photo of the ascetic is an imprint and has a frequency and a signature in creation, beyond the realities of varying cultures. If this photograph, which carries a Thought Radiation across time and space, is shown to an indigenous individual, there is most likely going to be a response. The image will both carry and automatically activate a link in time/space to our Christian ascetic. As a result, the radiation of love, light and compassion associated with Christ will bring forth a symbolic resonance in the myth of our indigenous observer.

Likewise, the same result would occur if the photograph were taken of a shaman, or a Hindu or a Buddhist holding the vision of the god form relevant to the Dream of each. They are all anchoring a portal of light in the matrix of the Dream. *The point here is that thought has, in this and any similar instance, had an impact beyond the time/space continuum and is activated by resonant intent and inner plane unity.* All this takes place within the Dream. The Dream is a matrix and the matrix holds all potential.

This is a much higher level thought transference than the earlier example.

One way in which all of Thought Projection and Thoughtform Linkage is used in creation is often disregarded, if not scorned at, by the culturally unaware Souls. A thoughtform may carry specific intent and be carried across time and space to a particular recipient. Such carrier thoughtforms inhabit the full inner world matrix and are coded frequencies that can, and do, act for better or worse. They are very specific and they are directed.

For better, these act in the field of white magic. For worse, the answer is obvious. They represent black magic and all the like which exist within the lower spectrum of human experience. Here the message is simple. One must seek to rise above the lower level constructs of the inner world, many of which we experience from the Dream of Mass Cultural Hypnosis. Mass marketing is a form of magic, in that it utilizes symbols, sound, light and color to form a relationship between the observer and the observed. This level uses Thought Linkage. The whole of the lower vibratory world is hyperlinked at the level of thought. In most instances a product or belief system (political or religious for instance) is projected and specific behavior follows. Thought Radiance is so much grander, higher and more joyfully embracing than any use of Thought Projection, for any purpose. It is to this end that we move forward.

Be Empty Before You Think

"People are like stained-glass windows. They sparkle and shine when the Sun is out, but when the darkness sets in, their true beauty is revealed only if there is a light from within."
Elizabeth Kübler-Ross, author of **On Death and Dying**

As we reveal these many layers of the Dream's construction, we equally uncover the many layers of our quest. We have noted how we create and that we can create anew our Dream. Surely all have witnessed the power of thought, but perhaps never before considered it in this way. Now we can. We may not yet know what the Power is that precedes the Dream, the Power Before Thought, but we do know that we can tap this power both individually and collectively, as One, to change our reality. We are asking questions and we want to know what we can do to build a greater Dream for the Greater Good.

So you ask, "How do I begin?" Simple practice gets us started. We know that our reality is a thought construct. Hence it is important for us to choose our thoughts with care. We must question our thinking at all times and question the source point of our thinking. Ask, "What am I thinking? Is this my own personality driven thought? Is this thought one I have accepted from global or local mass projection? Is this thought leading me to the Greater Good? Is this thought leading me towards health, harmony and peace?" There are many questions to choose, but all require Self Reflective Consciousness. This is contemplation of the flow of thought lines as they pass through your being. This is about being the Observer and watching, gracefully, as each thought passes through your stream of awareness. This is also about not investing time, energy or effort into empowering any thought that is deemed counter-productive to the Self. Great power comes from this Self-reflective query. This almost seems too simplistic, but it isn't. It is the first step of Self-reflection that offers tremendous creative potential for change as we take greater steps. It represents the first of three powerful keys to the process of knowing the Dream behind the Dream, behind the Dream, behind the Dream...*The Great Work.*

A SIMPLE QUEST

As a preemptor to revealing the process you can choose to work with to reach our goal, I am drawn to share a story from my early childhood. This was previously presented in my earlier volume, *Initiation Into Miracles*, and it has a significant role to play here as well. In my very early childhood, from around the age of five onwards, I would always go to bed with both a prayer and a question on my mind. I would say a prayer of sorts, requesting blessings for everyone ranging from my folks, brother, aunts, uncles, to pets, friends and beyond. It would stretch out to include the whole world by the time I had gotten close to the end. Then, as I approached the conclusion, I would also say a prayer for God. I know it sounds crazy, but it was really very simple. It was, simply put, "Bless Yourself Lord, whoever and whatever You are." That would get me to thinking. If God existed, then where did He/She come from? Something, greater, had to be *behind* the God I was praying to.

It makes sense if you think about it, not that I was being sensible at the time. Just plain inquisitive of the cosmic scheme. Once I had prayed for the God behind the God, I found myself confronted with the same dilemma. The God behind the God also had to have come from somewhere. So there had to be a Greater God, right?

This process occupied my mind for a considerable time until something uniquely beautiful would take place. Without fail, each and every night, I would take the same journey. I would lose consciousness of being who I knew myself to be. It was a process of disintegration of the lower self and the awakening of something much higher. Initially, it would begin with a separation of a part of myself (Astral) from my Physical Body. I would roll out into the expanse of light and travel the Universe. As I became more adept at this (and knew nothing of why it should not be so), I found I could accomplish the same result, much quicker, and reach into higher more profound states of peace and harmony. In the end, there were no thoughts of self. I had simply merged to a place of peace where thoughts and awareness of the manifestation of the Dream were not part of the broad spectrum of light that I had become.

It was, and still remains, a great place to *Be*. My reason for sharing this with you is quite straightforward. Society today, in just about all its forms, does not encourage us to ask questions. The real push is made for a "numbing down" of consciousness, along with an acceptance of physical reality and the religions of separation. Closely aligned with this and equally supported is our collective bathing in the matrix of the old age of fear, poverty, and all of its children. What I am about to ask you to consider is really very simple. If you actually take it to heart, you will activate the timeless wisdom that allows you to know who you truly are. You will peel back the layers of thought that come *after* the Power Before Thought. To do this will eventually place you nicely *within* the field of the Power Before Thought.

LOOKING AT THE KEYS

Practice Discernment in Thinking

Because we have the power of the Dreamer within us, we can choose to imagine and visualize our way back to the Dreamer - *to dream our way back to the Dreamer.* The first steps to touching the Power Before Thought utilize a simple, yet important, Self-reflective process. All Mystery Schools teach these keys as a precursor to accessing the deeper wisdom of Self. Firstly, we must practice the art of *Discernment in Thinking.* If you want to touch the Power Before Thought you must clear the matrix of your Soul of all the cobwebs that block the way. The discerning process is one of seeking always to track the source of any thought back to its origin. When you have tracked the origin, it is then important to comprehend why it strayed into your field of awareness. With the thought before you, ask yourself, "Did I draw it in by magnetic attraction of unhealed aspects of my Being? Is there an aspect of my Soul that needs help to heal? If so what is it and what must be done?"

Discernment implies a deep look at the flow of these thoughts and also a complete acceptance of responsibility for them. They *are* your thoughts, even if you did not act as their progenitor. When you have tracked their origin, I suggest that you track them *forward* - right through time/space - and ask yourself what the consequences of such thoughts have been and/or would be in your life? Be thorough. Once these answers start coming forth, recall always the work we have done together to this point. Remember that you are capable of *projecting, linking* and *radiating!* Ask yourself, "How will these thoughts, of which I am now aware, play out in the grand scheme of the Greater Good? Are they lower vibratory energies that simply add to the mass of cultural confusion and dismay? Will I act as a projector to others with similar issues in their lives that I have in my own? Will I be an image, a holding pattern, for others to touch and then open a hyperlink into a field of experience they can well do without?"

You see, all of these questions are part and parcel of discernment. The answers are not in the spectrum of yes, no, black or white. You are consciously choosing to create inside the Dream. You are taking action to clear the matrix of lower thoughts. You are acting within the field of ethics (your own) to harmonize the myth by which you live. Then you will act to tap into the magic of the Logos, the sacred geometric pattern of a dynamic and vibrant Soul. Once there, you have the capacity to move to the Source of the Dream. We are still not there yet, but we are getting closer - there is work to be done! You are now working with the beingness of the Human. This is Self Reflective Consciousness at work.

Question The Master

The second key you may successfully implement in this process is to *Question the Master*. Always question those who proffer "absolute" teachings – test the teacher. This questioning applies equally to anything you have read in this book. As I have stated many times, this book is no more than a suggestion. Your life is a suggestion. If you grasp anything as an absolute you will have collapsed the opportunity to expand and grow into the fullness of your Being. Keep all options open. The best teachers I have had all insisted that I question. This is the essence of the *mystical quest:* To embark upon a journey and to seek by questioning all that one is shown, told of and experienced in the field.

When an authority comes before you waving absolutes, be prepared to crush them and move through the ashes, like a phoenix rising to a new level of awareness - courtesy of the shoulder ride given by the one you questioned. No teacher should ever be the absolute. Ever! Each teaching from each master is but a pearl in a string of thoughts, presented many times by the teacher, eloquently, in a manner which conjures up images representative of myriad probable outcomes in the mind of the student. This is Thought Projection from the master.

If, on the other hand, you are graced to find a master who simply *radiates*, and you feel something bigger and more profound than you alone have ever felt in your life, then something else is unfolding. You have received a great gift. The place you then enter, in this instance, is into discernment. You ask, "What is this I am feeling?" Go deeper and deeper in the quest until you peel back the layers. You will reach a point where you will touch the master's radiance in a rich and ineffable manner. Once there you are on your way to revealing The Power Before Thought! When you find such a master being as this in your life you will recognise them by at least two attributes. Firstly, they demand that you question them. Secondly, they demand that when you have ascertained the authenticity and integrity of their beingness you move through their forms, and all they represent to you, to that which is before their forms. They must want you to not be attached to their forms but rather to reach out to the Power before the thought of their forms.

The Power Before Thought

Challenge The Delusion Of Mass Cultural Hypnosis

The third key offered to us is one so very often ignored completely! On the quest we must *Challenge the Delusion of Mass Cultural Hypnosis*. In order to prevent our acceptance of delusional images as reality, in a rapidly evolving spectrum of consciousness, we must reign in delusional imaginings. I use the word "must" intentionally, because I (as a teacher, not a master) have found these three points of discipline to be priceless keys to the path of dreaming our way back to the Dreamer and re-creating our Dream. The matrix of our reality is a composite of streams of thought. Each, as we have stated, is either created by our own Souls from the Source or is projected upon our Souls by the multi-dimensional universe in which infinite aspects of our selves take up residence.

The critical importance of this key can be seen clearly by observing the work of channels and psychics. I am not diminishing this activity in so saying, for I have no right to judge, nor would I want to. Yet even a cursory exploration into these fields reveals quickly that some practitioners have applied the keys we speak of to their own work while some have clearly not. This is a useful example to us in distinguishing between the tone of mastery and the tone of fantasy in our dreaming within the Dream.

A psychic will act as a vessel to tune in to the forces of imagery, sensitivity and perception from the inner realm. Very few if any ever go near the Power Before Thought, and most operate in the lower realm of Mythos. By not questioning and allowing our imaginations to run wild, we often propagate the experience of separation by accepting what we are told as absolute. We must use discernment. Discernment is necessary as we observe the message received or given, and we must look at the manner in which another Soul's imagination has tapped into images that our Souls have accepted as true. These images may be self-reflected by the psychic, or may be simply self-limiting through their unquestioning acceptance of the images.

One thing is for sure. Today, in each moment, we witness countless episodes of Souls engaged in the Dream who have not discerned their very own thoughts, let alone those of others. They have strewn fanciful and untested imaginings of grandeur along their paths for entertainment. This is a sure fire way to cloud up the matrix and block the path of easy access to the Power before the thought that generated these delusions. I suggest that you never allow yourself to get caught in this energy. By all means, test and experience it if you wish, but I encourage you to be ever mindful that you are *greater* than all of the projections passing through your stream of awareness.

Mastery of the human experience is ultimately about clarity of thought. Clarity of thought brings discernment of energy associated with inner world perceptions. This, in turn, leads to the dispelling of all imaginings that are less than productive and leads us, ultimately, to inner world guidance of quality.

IT'S A BATTLE OUT THERE SO STAY WITHIN!

You might have noticed that we have dropped down to the

everyday level of the Dream from the lofty heights we were previously exploring - it's genesis, "beginning", or Creation points. We have journeyed through many dimensions of the Dream together, and we understand that we must know of the Dream in order to change the Dream. This means that we must understand the mechanisms the Dream uses to perpetuate itself...

with our help of course! These mechanisms are those that wield the power of thought throughout Creation.

For as long as we exist within the Dream, so also will perceptions of separation and duality. These are the primary thoughtforms that generate the possibility of images and symbols which represent white and black, day and night, good and evil, and so forth. These primary divisions within the spectrum of thought are what we implement to build our reality. They require our awareness so we can change them. *They are not, however, our truth, and neither do they represent our nature. They are merely thoughtforms within the Dream. They are projections, linkages and radiances.*

Yet whilst we engage the Dream at this everyday level, we can ascertain that the human experience is one constantly engaged in an inner battle. It is a battle between the polarities created within the Dream. The polarity between what we consider to be "ethically" good, right or beneficial to humanity and what we consider to be the opposite. For many it is deemed to be a battle between good and evil.

This battle, at the physical level, tears apart the physical human, moment by moment, as the individual engages in a balancing act to bring forth the good. Yes, all serve to bring forth the good. For even those who may be labeled as bad, evil, and corrupt are engaged inside the Dream for the purposes of bringing forth the good.

At a higher level - in the field of the Soul - this battle revolves around the myths that we hold to be true. These are the projections we direct at each other of thoughtforms in a desire for control, with groups of us doing the same for mass control. "My way is correct, yours is wrong. I can justify this and that because I have access to the Truth." We have heard it all before, but where has it gotten us?

At the level of Spirit the battle reaches a higher level and involves the Logos. These are the parts of ourselves that architecturally engineer the thoughtforms that the Soul projects and the Physical Body adopts as absolute, tying them to time and space.

Moving beyond the Spirit battles, we leave the world of thoughtform and enter the world of Thought Radiance. The highest thought, the most powerful thought, is that of the One. It is beyond right and wrong and any battle. It is the radiant Power Before Thought.

The Power Before Thought radiates from the highest non-local, non-linear, timeless here and now through all aspects of all beings, at all times in all places. It expresses its greatness through the field of Being! This field of Being co-exists within and is yet greater than the Dream itself. It is a non-definitive, indescribable, sentient presence that is, in itself, the means through which the Dream has acted as a vehicle for great expansion of this Power Before Thought into places where it may never have been expressed had that part of us chosen not to take it there.

However, as we move into the density of the imaginary constructs of time and space, we adopt a relationship to the lower dimensions as reality, and we build structures that block the free flow of the light of radiance. The Sun will shine directly on all, regardless of race, creed or culture. If we build a place of worship, as holy as it might be, we must still introduce artificial light to replace that which is natural. The Sun is blocked and we live inside the shadow. The light inside is now that of lower level thoughtforms inhabited by human fears and linked to a desire for control.

Here we come face to face with the need to really take stock of what we can do to bring forth the radiance once more and dissolve the thoughtforms that have kept us locked inside the prison of our own making. It is time to BE Human and allow the Dream to be cleansed of fear and all of its ancestors and family members.

Then, and only then, can the Power Before Thought take root in the human heart. Then, and only then, can the true Power Before Thought be directed by the essence of your Being into the manifestation of the Greater Good...for your life and all others, for all are One with you.

The Power Before
Thought

82

11

Life Is A Game, Play It

"There are only two ways to live your life. One is as though nothing is a miracle. The other is as though everything is a miracle."
Albert Einstein

Being Real is a challenge worth taking. To "Be Real" does not mean to "get real", in the colloquial sense. Far from it. To be *real* is literally that. Being Real. The beingness is to detach from the humanness as the driving force. The reality is to realize that nothing is real in any way. All is a suggestion. Therefore, to be real is to look upon all of creation as being changeable, transient and liquid. The only reality that can exist is the unchangeable. That which is unchangeable is beyond death and manipulation. It is unknowable, for to "know it" implies a perception of separation. In other words, if we were to "know it" we would be using part of ourselves to identify, quantify and qualify what we observe. Anything we can do this to is not real. It is in our Dream. It is when we reach beyond that process of measurement and identification that we actually become real. It is then that we realize we do not know God. We can know the teachings of great master beings but not know God. We can only know in the sense that we dissolve into an identity-less state of Being. Hence, Being Real. How do we get there, in context of our journey thus far?

An old adage of spiritual wisdom tells us, *"Life is a game and we must learn to play it."* It is not just any game, but one that is choreographed by the Power we are constantly referring to, the Source of all radiance. If we become severely strict and static in our dance with life energies, we move into contraction and even death. Do you know, here and now, where and how you are playing the game? Most certainly you are playing it multi-dimensionally. To get the best results, therefore, you will need to think multi-dimensionally.

Expand your horizons and move beyond the linear structures that bind you. To do this you will need to understand how the game unfolds in different dimensions of the Dream. We need to consider how the ultimate radiance emanating from the Power Before Thought, acting through the field of beingness, plays out through different dimensions.

PLAYING IN THE ĐIMENSIONS

Third dimensional reality is relatively heavy duty for many of us. The third dimensional experience is one that is richly embraced by the vehicle of the Physical Body, linear time/space and ethics. The physical Dream is one of separation. The game has rules that always seem to change in such a way that we are prevented from reaching our goals. It is a dimension of polarity, limitation and separation of self from others. Great unreality exists inside this dimension. It is a dimension of lack, victim-consciousness and unworthiness; it is filled with shame, guilt, and all their cousins. True love, cooperation and joy are missing from this dimension.

"What?" you say, "But I experience joy and love!" If you experience love, cooperation and joy, they are not of this dimension. They are filtering through the field of radiance, through the field of Being, as the Power, into lower levels of the Dream. This is good news! For once we know how to recognize and work with the filters we can change the way we play the game.

All of the life-contracting qualities listed above are no more or less than structured thoughtforms that perpetuate the continuance of an illusionary reality. They are unreal. But as long as we remain fixed inside a lower vibrational state of Being, no amount of magical powers and revelation will help us play the game with joy. You have already received some of the clues as to how you can lift your vibration. The effective use of the three key tools in the last chapter alone will start the process for you. *You will begin to recognize radiance as distinct from projection and linkage.* This is a major step up the ladder of liberation and love.

REACHING THE HIGHER LEVELS

When we rise above the third dimension we begin to delineate the Dream into layers of experience. This is all well and good, as long as we remain aware, at all times, that we are still in the Dream. In the *lower fourth dimension,* we engage the vehicle of the Soul, experiencing time as is stipulated in our model, and form concrete structures of consciousness out of the myths that we accept as truth. The predominant thoughtforms are supportive of separation, battle and distress. If you feel energies of anxiety, distress, fear, and the like, be ever mindful that you *are not* these energies and neither are you limited by them. There are parts of your Self, sentient and alive in the lower fourth dimension, which may be lost aspects of your Self that were torn away during times of crisis (sentient and alive like Joan's spiritual dog). They may be from this lifetime or any number of previous lifetimes, all of which are resident in the here and now.

Astral entities have their high residence in this dimension and play their games of manipulation with our vulnerable Soul aspects. This is the realm of magic, which unlocks the qualities of the psyche, intuitive knowing and feminine feelings. Culturally, we tend not to trust the positive nature of these qualities. We often call on "coincidence" to answer for something far deeper. It feels right to see things this way. Why? Because Thought Linkages and Thought Projections support and reaffirm this answer when we ask, "What just happened here? What did I just experience?" These qualities of feeling are at least fourth-dimensionally activated. *Remember, you actually do function here all the time, as you so do in all dimensions simultaneously. It is the act of collapsing our awareness into a reality that prevents our knowing of these multi-dimensional selves.*

This is a most significant point. All of humanity is psychic, all of humanity is intuitive, and feminine qualities are active in all of humanity in its higher vibrational state. Yet not all of humanity is attuned to these qualities, and therefore it is very easy to give ourselves over to the lower vibrational fields of astral entities that may seek to manipulate our Souls in times of vulnerability. It is key that we always but always seek Truth and never sacrifice Truth at the altar of any form of Mass Cultural Hypnosis or to any astral entity that portends to deliver "absolutes". Remain aware and test your teachers. Great points of Truth will often pierce the veil that we have artificially constructed to keep us separate from higher radiance of the Power. These points of Truth may likewise break through the veil courtesy of the intervening radiance of an authentic teacher. Recall here our exploration of radiance. A true teacher will radiate the higher vibrations and you will feel the Truth.

The higher dimensions open before us fields of greater possibilities. The Dream expands and we become more aligned with our beingness. The personality-driven modality of the lower third dimension gives way to the *higher fourth dimension* and ultimately aligns with the richness of the *lower fifth dimension*. This is where great radiance comes forth. It is in this dimension that the light of your heart, as One with the Power, begins to shine through. All great mystics, masters and teachers playing inside the Dream radiate their potent teachings forth from this sacred light. When this high radiance of light shines through the veils of the shadows constructed in the minds of men inside the Dream, great magic occurs. Unreality falls away, and along with it so do the infinite thoughtforms that no longer hold sway under the light of the rich, abiding Power that precedes all thought.

When you dance in this dimension you realize without doubt that you are not your Physical, Emotional or Mental Body. You realize that you are indeed greater than all and any combination thereof. The Dreamer is within you and the Dreamer is the Source that is beyond you. Nothing can happen outside of your will or desire. True free will lies in Being the beingness of the One. Words and explanations no longer suffice. Reality shines through and dissolves the barriers that prevent our knowing our beingness.

PRAYING FOR A MIRACLE?

Right now, at this moment in linear time, a genuine movement from the unreal to the real is transpiring. A dissolution of the lower dimensional aspects of the Dream is occurring. This shift implies that we have collectively accessed the path of Self-realization by way of an intensification of Self Reflective Consciousness. The events we have choreographed into creation have now, through all races, creeds and cultures, drawn us into a place of transition: Lower Dream to Higher Dream and upwards and beyond. It is a mergence of *Personality* with *Soul*, edging further and deeper into a mergence of *Soul* and *Spirit*. Boundaries are falling away and creation is becoming more and more expansive. The apparent contractions before us are no more than gifts from our Being, offering us a chance to expand - to change from the changeable to the changeless.

The journey is one of magic, mystery and mastery. These are accompanied along the way by miracles, until a point at which miracles can simply no longer exist. Because a miracle, for all intents and purposes, is believed to be associated with God and God's divine rule, and as such it remains a construct of the Dream. If viewed from the higher levels of Spirit, however, we reach a richer understanding of what a miracle truly is. In the words of St. Thomas Aquinas, "There is no such thing as a miracle. What we call a miracle is simply our lack of understanding of God's law." God's law is, for all intents and purposes, also a construct within the Dream of humanity. So why do we pray for miracles?

THERE ARE NO MIRACLES

A miracle implies a suspending of the laws that govern time and space to bring about an outcome that would otherwise contradict those laws. Pretty straightforward when you think about it. Miracles are not possible when we are bound by the constructs of our own limited thinking. For instance, with regularity, doctors encounter spontaneous remission of terminal illness in their practice of medicine. Some doctors with a vested interest in their careers as surgeons may even find a way to disprove it. If, however, we place the same doctors in a life-altering scenario, in which they suffer from a terminal illness, the chances are that time and space may alter enough to allow for the possibility of a miracle. Why? Because the belief and will of the doctors change.

Rising up to the highest levels of the Dream and beyond does not mean there is no longer a Dream. To leave the Dream altogether means absorption, or mergence, into the Dreamer and beyond. If we engage in the Dream, as a Dreamer and director, then the "unreality" we call a miracle disappears, because we are the choreographer of the elements. We dictate time/space. We ourselves are the Dreamer bringing forth the collapse of time and space. Instantaneous healings, coincidences and happenings that "should not" happen (according to Classical Newtonian Physics) come to pass with regularity and ease. From this perspective we no longer need miracles - we are the miracle! Healing serves no purpose to us, for we are no longer suffering fragmentation. The Power that is before thought is the Power that manifests the miracles - at all levels of Being.

12

You Never Went Anywhere

"I will not let anyone walk through my mind with their dirty feet."
Mohandas Gandhi

Reaching through time and space to find what we seek in this life can at times seem a long somewhat tiring journey! Many who share with me during healing sessions ask, "What is my purpose?", or a question of similar theme. Yet people do not visit a healer simply to know their purpose. They visit to unlock the door that allows them to *become* their purpose. Knowing is unreal without Being.

Hidden within this query is a desire expressed by most Souls at some point in their lives. This is the desire to know that, regardless of our lives' varied pathways, we have made a difference to the lives of those with whom we share, to the world, and to ourselves. For we all want to have lived a meaningful life. Beneath the veils of the Dream we use to cover ourselves lies this deep-seated desire. You might laugh, but if we think about it, even the demon of Dan Brown's novel *Inferno*, Bertrand Zobrist, wants to be remembered for having done something that had a profoundly positive impact upon humanity! Albeit his idea may seem dark and shrouded in all manner of ethical issues: The release of a plague that would cull the over-population of humans and allow a rebuilding of civilization is surely ethically questionable. Yet the point remains. Every Being is created within our Dream. This character was created in Brown's Dream to discuss and explore the polarities of making a difference: Feed the masses and give medicine that will help them live to a great age, or release a toxic plague and help the future generations rebuild a firm civilization.

PLAYING YOUR CARDS RIGHT

Each player in human history has played the same cards of duality. We play this game inside ourselves every moment. We make choices and decisions as to where we place our consciousness. Yet all the while we play out this game of choice at the lower level, we abdicate our role as the timeless Beings we truly are. Oftentimes this abdication is no more choice than a surrender to the cultural hypnosis we yield to. Even so we must play, but in doing so we must never lose sight of the fact that *we are all of the players and the choreographer as well.* Making a difference is very important, not just to humanity at large, but ultimately to the Self. For in essence, your Self is the Dream and your Self is choosing to play the game. When we transform all of the apparent issues that trouble the Dream at large, so too do we transform the Self. And, conversely, when we transform the Self, so too are transformed all the troubling issues within the Dream.

To reach this sacred place of being, to cross what is so often portrayed as the "final frontier" of duality and separation, requires a willingness to integrate all that we have explored herein and dispel the lower vibrational energies that link us to that which we don't want. It is a process of detachment, letting go and reclamation of all parts of Being. It is a collective urge within one's greater Self to breathe with ease for all parts of one's Soul. To allow the Spirit to feed the Soul, and the Soul to direct the personality within the Dream. This Soul-direction leads us out of the illusion and into a space where abundance, health, well-being, inner peace and joy are all achievable, not by effort, but by awakening - by mastery of the Dream from a point of Being, of Being the Dreamer.

This is the point of actually Being the Awakened Heart, the Buddha, the Great Spirit, the Source, the Christ or the Krishna. We can call this point by many names, for in naming it we give it meaning in our Dream. *The important thing is that we recognize this Point of our Beingness as the Dreamer beyond the Dream!* For all of these are names, and as sacred names they are fields of power. *The resonant frequency of all of them is, in essence, the same.* (Remember the image of our meditating Christian ascetic and the indigenous Soul who felt his devotion through the photograph?) The personalization of each form is what generates the separation that keeps us from unifying all parts of our Being and returning to centre.

THE IMAGE OF THE FORMLESS

From the Self-reflective perspective of Being One with the formless Dreamer, and knowing the great power conveyed by thoughtform as image, we find ourselves gifted a true understanding of the power of sacred image in the creation of the Dream. Many are the images around this world that portray great beings who have stepped foot upon the Earth, over the ages, to teach us a higher truth. These images of Buddha, Christ, Mary and other masters are equally supported by images of the Sun, the light, the void and other similar constructs. We might ask, "Why do we meditate or gaze upon these? Is it just to make us feel good? Is it a religious requirement?" Certainly the latter may be so in many spiritual traditions, but this does not hold true for followers of Islam, as an example, because they have no form upon which to place their faith. Neither do the followers of Judaism. No, there is actually a different answer to our query.

Recall once again our meditating Christian ascetic and his interaction with the indigenous Soul, and you will start to piece this together. Remember also our discussion of my client who had streams of consciousness tied to his Soul through photographic images, and you will get an even greater insight. If you think of Joan's imaginary pet dog that has followed her throughout her lifetime, the puzzle will get clearer. If you then think of all of these in context of the images being created inside the Dream every second of our existence, at all levels of Being, the light bulb will go on. The reasons people meditate upon such images are multiple and all are revealed using the clues we have explored throughout this journey.

Firstly, sacred images are counter-posed against images of dark, violent or chaotic energy. Each has a field effect. Choosing the latter brings forth entrenchment *in* the power of thought. These images take hold and toss you around the lower levels of the Dream. Images of the former variety, the icons of all spiritual tradition, bring about a major elevation of our Being - back into a field of Pure Radiance. Not all images of avatars and sacred beings are equal, of course. Those of a suffering Christ are supportive of guilt, anger, pain, suffering, and so forth. Those of a tubby Buddha bring up all manner of energy associated with obesity, etc. However, all the higher images, in their color, symbology, depictions and composition, act to the discerning Soul, not the personality, as a catalytic converter. They propel the Soul away from the lower Dream and push it into the higher reaches of radiance.

These images proffer great comfort to the angst-ridden "separate" Soul. Such is the power of these images. They dispel anxiety and uncertainty, which comes from fear and separation. Why? Because they are beacons to the greater light. They are *not* the greater light, but they are *pointers* as to getting there without the calamity and fears of the lower thought world. Remember the master's words: "Come test and question. Then when you think you have the answers, GO THROUGH THIS FORM." Such radiant images also fulfill a part of ourselves so often tempted and drawn in by Mass Cultural Hypnosis, causing us to become attached and believe that we need what we don't in order to survive in the Dream. These radiant fields also fortify our Spirit to climb up and above the desires that are constantly being projected to us in the manner of thoughtforms. Such desires, if not culled by an act of discernment, automatically and similarly tend to weaken our resolve and act as clouds blocking our connection to The Power Before Thought - the Power before Radiance.

Given the clear benefits offered through the presence of sacred images, irrespective of the truth of the tradition from which they are sourced, it is well worth having them around us to shift the energy in our homes and work environments. To access this pathway of clearing, you can simply find any uplifting energetic prints and symbols you resonate with. They will also help purify the mind of the constant bombardment of thoughtforms that come from daily life.

Such purification is not a religious purification, for that brings with it conditions and servitude. Rather it is a transformative purification whereby one can become addicted to the freedom of thought and the wonder of being shackle free. Such a purifying process prepares you for the possibilities of "rolling out" at nighttime and entering the universe at large. When this takes place you are, without doubt, aware once and for all that you are *in* the world but not *of* the world. The radiant Power then works through you. The more you clear the greater your expansion. The radiant Power Before Thought feeds all higher potentials, and so much more.

There is, however, one proviso that will greatly assist your grasp of this in the way that can help you most. It is important that you understand this vital point: If you are to truly touch the Power Before Thought, as you will, you must keep constant awareness upon the knowing that *you are playing the game inside the field of Maya*. You are literally an agent, if you will, spreading the Power of Radiance in the field of the Dream. How you spread it, where you spread it, and why you spread it is all Maya. Maya is a dream in itself. If we fail to recall this, we can suffer enormously inside the Dream by grasping at the unreal and manifesting the "un-realities" of poverty, angst, hunger and so forth.

A DREAM WITHIN A DREAM

There is a beautiful story taken from the many teaching stories surrounding the incarnation of Lord Krishna that illustrates the meaning of what we have shared here quite perfectly. Though this story involves Lord Krishna, one certainly need not be a devotee of Krishna, nor any other divine form, to grasp and gain insight from the Truth of the teaching offered. You might think of Krishna as a teacher of great radiance who awakens your own Dreamer within. Such would be the awakening offered through the teachings of many great beings throughout "time". We do well to leave the judgments of culture aside and engage the story for the pearls of wisdom to be found. Though one may find varying versions of this tale, I will share it the way it is best understood. As you read through this keep in mind our starting point in this book - Maya. To do so helps you see the timeliness of our time and the importance of our thoughts and that which precedes them.

The timeless sage Narada, known to be free of Maya and able to play above the lower Dream, is blessed to move without limitation through all dimensions. The relationship between Narada and Lord Krishna was so deep and intimate that Narada, the son of the Creator (Lord Brahma), was empowered to explore the rich depths of Creation accompanied by Lord Krishna Himself. One day, while busy walking and talking with Lord Krishna, Narada decided to ask Krishna for an experience that had been denied to him – the experience of Maya.

After quiet reflection upon his request, Krishna informed Narada that given the abundance of blessings he enjoyed, it would without doubt be a pointless exercise for him to delve into Maya. Narada, however, persisted, and Krishna conceded, agreeing that Narada be allowed to experience Maya. Prior to His commencement of the experience, Krishna suggested that they take a moment to lie down and rest. At that point, Krishna asked Narada to fetch Him a cup of water to satisfy His thirst. Narada immediately stood up from under the shade of the tree in the divine garden and wandered off in search of water for Lord Krishna.

Narada walked out into the fields, enjoying the Sun as its rays poured down upon him. After a lengthy walk he noticed that the Sun's heat was becoming intolerable. He thought to himself that he should acquire a greater volume of water. With that thought in mind he noted a small community some distance away, near the horizon, towards which he moved at a fairly rapid pace.

Eventually he arrived outside the front door of one of the village houses. When the door opened he was struck into a zone of ecstatic bliss! Before him stood the most beautiful young woman he had ever seen or imagined could exist. Her beauty mesmerized him. This was all new to him, and he enjoyed the experience fully. As he looked upon her, the idea (as yet unformed or created as Maya) passed through his consciousness that he should take her to be his wife. His thoughts ran wild with ideas of how much more beautiful this blessed young woman was than any of the wives of any of the gods. Truly, he believed, there was no god with a wife so beautiful as this. He therefore, with no further consideration, simply asked her to become his wife.

The young woman was somewhat taken aback by Narada's request. "Aren't you Narada, the great sage?" she asked. "Indeed" he replied. "Then I shall certainly accept your hand in marriage if my father approves," she said. "I will wait until he returns," Narada joyfully replied. A few days later the father returned and to his amazement observed Narada in his house. He questioned what had brought Narada there, only to hear a request for his daughter's hand in marriage. The father was mystified as to why such a great sage, one who is free of Maya and able to explore all dimensions should wish to desire such a bond. The father explained to Narada that if he were indeed to marry his daughter then Narada would be required to stay at home and surrender his blessing to freely explore the entire Dream without bond or limit. He would be required to surrender the freedom he has enjoyed and assume full responsibility for the marriage and all that it would bring. Narada, without hesitation, agreed. The marriage took place and life settled into a routine in the family home, in the picturesque community.

Within some time his wife gave birth to their first child, followed closely by yet another. Happiness abounded in their home. Their world expanded to include a social circle of friends of the family and they partook in all the activities of their social circle. Then one day Narada stepped outside the door to notice that a huge storm was developing on the horizon, the likes of which he had never previously seen. The clouds were dark and the atmosphere was thick with pending peril. Then the rains came and in a short time precipitated a flood. Narada without a second thought told his wife and children and informed that they needed to leave immediately and head to higher ground.

As they moved away from the now flooded home, the water level rose faster than they could escape. Soon their first-born was swept away in the waters. Shortly thereafter, their second child suffered the same fate. Then, as Narada raced his wife of such beauty to the higher reaches, her foot became trapped and she also was washed away from him. Alone now, Narada struggled to reach the higher ground. Upon arriving he sat there, under a tree, weeping. He had seen the entire community swept away. His entire beloved family was gone. He sat all alone, distraught. He was also very angry at Krishna, his Lord, who had allowed all of this to transpire. Narada sank deep into his misery. The tears, anger, rage, grief, sadness, and even hatred for Krishna reached a boiling point. He knew Krishna had abandoned him in a time of great need. This most loving merciful God, the Lord of Lords, had forsaken him and allowed him to suffer. Never again, he railed, would he pay homage to this "false god". Such was his pain.

In the midst of this turmoil, Narada felt a hand on his shoulder and looked up to see Krishna standing there. Before he could say a word Krishna asked him, "Narada, where is my cup of water?" Narada launched into an expression of rage, but as he did so he looked around and saw that he was exactly where he started his journey - in the garden, under the tree, with Krishna. It had all been a Dream. Krishna smiled. "Water?" He asked. Narada then realized exactly what Maya truly is. Krishna smiled and blessed him that he should never have to return into the field of Maya - to the Dream! The blessings of Pure Love had been revealed to Narada. To have been in the Dream, but not off the dream. Such was the grace.

ARE YOU NOT NARADA?

Narada here represents the timeless Divine Spark. That part of us that, though individual, knows it is One with the Dreamer (Krishna). It is his desire to enter the realm of creation within Maya that propels him into emotional turmoil. So lost is he in the Dream that he becomes unaware of the passage of time. Birth, death, and all that each brings to us passes through him. It is only when the touch of Krishna comes to him that he realizes he has fallen victim to Maya. To the Dream! He had surrendered to the illusion of a lesser truth and gotten caught up in the drama. Why did he do this? Because he wanted the experience. Why do we do this? Because we want the experience! When did it stop for Narada? When he had had enough. When will it stop for any of us? When we too realize that we have had enough, and that it is upon us to reclaim our birthright as timeless Beings - birthed before even Narada. As the Lord Buddha so expediently observed, *it is the Soul's involvement in time and space that brings suffering.*

We live in the Dream and we must continue to play our role in the Dream, but with wisdom we can play differently. With the knowing of who we truly are we can play the game with greater detachment and with the moment by moment release of all that is projected upon us that we no longer want or need. We know the joy to be had in living the greater Dream for the Greater Good. Now we are ready to integrate all our understandings and to initiate, at all levels of our Being, beyond the constraints of time and space, the greatest journey of all and the creation of infinite higher possibilities for ourselves and all that is.

IV

Decoding A Secret

13

The Power Before Thought

"Only one thing I expect from all of you: to be yourself, to discover your inner beauty, your purity of consciousness, your hidden splendor - and spread it to as many people as possible. People are miserable. Help them to laugh a little, to sing a little, to dance a little."
Osho

We have taken this journey of exploration in search of the Power Before Thought - the Power behind all that we know to be the Dream of our creation. If we did not previously grasp our true nature, perhaps we now understand well that our radiant essence directs thoughts into creation. These thoughts are real forces - engineered by higher aspects of the One Self and brought forth into an array of physical, emotional and mental possibilities. We have "suggested" that our own power to engineer creation and enter into the highest levels of purity lies in detaching from lower vibrational thoughts and in purging these energies. This level of purity verges on the brink of dissolution. Reaching it may seem frightening, but it needn't be.

The brink is the end of duality and as such the final choice. When we cross that threshold, choice is withdrawn from our journey. We become magnetized to the thought-less realm of timeless purity. It is here that all forms are surrendered, and with them all attachments to emotions, beliefs, attitudes, past lives, future lives and all that is associated with these. In their place comes a wondrous experience that replaces the unreal with a reality tone that cannot be measured. This reality tone is the threshold, the "ring pass not" that we all, eventually, come face-to-face with at the point of transition from the physical form. Reaching it through conscious exploration, conscious detachment, and conscious Self-reflection empowers that which is behind and before the first thought to manifest as our Being. It is here, at this choice point, reached through our act of will and from our desire for the Greater Good to prevail, that we move into the realm of Self-mastery. Not before.

APPROACHING THE POWER

Getting to this point, however, is not about Self-mastery but rather self-mastery. This is our journey to the Power Before Thought – the Power that we have always been, awaiting our conscious activation. This is about letting go of the lower vehicles and reaching for the higher. Once there, at the threshold, we are gifted a vision of the deep Truth of the Dreamer – The Power we have called the Power Before Thought. Having journeyed through the Dream together to this point of understanding, it is now time to reveal the Truth of this Power.

This Power is Love. But it is not the love we think we know. Thinking that we know love is simply the automatic response that keeps us from experiencing exactly what I am about to share! This Love is not just any love. It is a unique embrace, and an immersion in and of love, that cannot be fathomed by the mind. Any endeavour to explain it is fraught with peril, for the Dream is filled with delusions that will capture us along the way and sidetrack us into irrelevances. These diversions subjugate the fire that burns deep within our heart to shed the shackles of *delusional love* and enthuse ourselves with the *Love of an Infinite Splendour* that is beyond comprehension. If I use the words I want to use right now, the trapdoor will open and you most certainly will fall in! Therefore, let me use a Sanskrit word to speak of this Love - a word which will hold little or no association to something already believed to be known by many of you. This word *does not describe the state*, but rather *leads us closer* to the ineffable stateless state we seek.

The Power Before Thought This word is *"Bhava"*. It has many variations of meaning, but for our purposes we will ascribe the following meaning to it, though it cannot actually be described or known through words. Bhava is the ecstatic, liberating, mindless expanse of total consciousness - Self surrender of individuality and all physical, emotional, mental, and spiritual energies into a focus on one-pointed devotion to the *Thoughtless Void*, the *pre-Dream state... The Power Before Thought*. Through this channel, this portal of one-pointed collapse of consciousness, there is a communion with a brilliance of infinite proportions. This Infinite Splendour is timelessly-emanating Love that is neither conditional nor unconditional. It is beyond being Pure.

It is, simply put, *Supreme Love*. Yet this alone is still an inadequate description. Try to think of it and it has slipped away from one's grasp. It is not a quantifiable entity in time/space. We can only explore how to realize it, to show you the Way. This is as the Lord Buddha did. He gave no discourse on absolutes, he simply showed the way. This is true of all great teachers. They can only show the way. No great master from any tradition specifically stated that He or She was the final resting place. "I Am the Way," is one mantra that could be applied to all. Including the great teachers of science and metaphysical studies. To each master being it is a stateless state - a Nirvana, Heaven, Loka. They were very clever *not* to define it. It is humanity, through its high priests, that has sought to define it, and in so doing keep us inside the recycled loop of the lower Dream. To us, who knows what it will be! It is, however, beneficial for us to consider what we can say about it rather than what it is. Remember though, the Way is not the final resting point.

THE RESIDENT IN OUR HEARTS

This Supreme Love of which we speak resides everywhere and nowhere. It is before, within and post thought. It is immanent and transcendent. For our purposes though, caught up as we are in the Mass Cultural Hypnosis of our illusionary time, we are limited to thinking of it as a place, or state, to which we aspire. Only then do we believe that we can become that state, place and being. *Supreme Love is the very Power that emanates forth the birth of thought.* It is latent within all of creation and lies dormant, as the inescapable driving force, to rediscover itself in its own true nature. It is in everything, closer than you could ever conceive of, and it resides, vibrates and emanates from focal points in the hearts of all creatures in all worlds.

This Supreme Love is the ultimate source of all universes, great and small. Every existence is found within. It is higher and grander than Being. Yes, more potent, beautiful, profound and joyful than the simple art of Being. It is beyond the nothingness that renders one unconscious to its presence as one travels the Way. Yet it is *the* Source that prevails upon the unconscious quality of all in the Dream to release, surrender, let go and become conscious on the path to full realization of its existence. It dissolves the human constructs of unconscious, sub-conscious, outer conscious, and super-conscious. They all are no more than the Dream. The path of their dissolution is mysterious and filled with opportunities of great discovery of love along the way. To expand into and become this Supreme Love, there can be no we – only *Thee*. No conditions. You must know that you are One with this Power.

"Unconditional love" is a human construct. Consequently, rarely do we look at the expanse of kingdoms that comprise the multitude of universes and dimensions and realize the essence of Love as the substratum in all kingdoms. All! The rocks, the trees, the insects, the wind, the Sun, the mountains, and the ocean. Supreme Love is the very foundation, the bedrock of all of these kingdoms, in all of their expressions, in all dimensions of existence, across all time/space possibilities. They have their

existence through this Power! This Power resides within you as Supreme Love, and when we can know, understand, and live that Truth, all of creation sings to the same chorus of light and joy. It is a one-pointed devotion to that which we *are* in our core. It is a Love like no other. It requires great discipline in the art of discernment. One must honor the vibration of one's Being in every thought, word and deed with a gentle yet potent reverence that invokes no field or vibratory engagement other than the Power. Fix the arrow of your heart on the mark of the Source.

HOW WILL I KNOW WHEN I AM GETTING THERE?

When this Supreme Love burns within you, in a state of restless stirring, you know the time has come. You will recognize it in your life. It will not be by the challenges that arise in life that reveal its closeness. Rather, it is the move to gentle tears you experience when you think or realize something simple and yet profound about another Soul. For instance, if a child is rescued by a team of dedicated police officers and you feel something, you are feeling the love for the child – this child is the child within you which is the child in the womb of all mothers. The same feelings are felt when you or another helps an elderly or sick person in need. Or if you, or others, feed the hungry or dance with an invalid and feel their smiles. You know it because you have experienced it. And yet, it subsides and life goes on. *You are not yet aware, but you are on the Way.* You are making progress. Slowly but surely you will begin to release the bonds of ignorance which tie you tightly to the sheaths of all lower dimensions built up within the lesser Dreams. All desires, links to, and involvement with dimensions of parallel lives will now start to dissolve. Even the thought of future lives and associated attachments fall away, taking with it the illusion of karma. This love, as it shifts and changes from raw conditional love, through to unconditional love, and into Supreme Love, will gently nurture and guide you all the Way.

Just a momentary (*Truti*) vision of the grandeur of this Power severs all the fetters and liberates the lesser self into the highest realm. One must be ready for it to show itself and then grasp it with an open heart. The Dreamer will play with you, like a loving parent plays with his or her child. He is the mystical One, the gatekeeper to the universe. He is the Light of lights, the fire of every Sun. No Sun illumines the Dreamer. It is He/She as the Supreme Love that illumines all suns, stars, solar systems, galaxies, and universes.

That which we call the Cosmos is the body and being of the Dreamer as the expression of Supreme Love. Devotion to mergence with this field of Supreme Love is the human journey into Beingness and beyond. It is Self-reflection on the Light that illumines all that takes one there. This light inside the Dream is reflected in infinite splendor across the heights and depths of creation. That of which we are ideationally engineered inside the Dream are the living, sentient elements of earth, water, fire, air and spirit. They too are Love.

Here I must ask, "How do you relate to them?" For they are your children. How can we judge them and not love them, in all of their expressions, as they have loved us? This is the Supreme Knowing. Supreme Love is eternal freedom, boundless and pervading all directions. When you know this, you awaken to this Supreme Love within. Then you are free! You are perfectly fulfilled in the ocean of Spirit and have no needs or wants. Here the master being stands in the height of a storm and commands the elements to obey. And they do.

HEART TO HEART

Can you honestly think of anything greater than not needing anything? Go on, try! I ask you, "If you do not need anything at all, literally nothing, what can you long for?" You cannot argue for something here, because to do so involves delving back into the Dream for the fear losing what you treasure in the Dream as real. There is fear and danger in love – human love. It is conditional and has its very basis built on cause and effect. Unconditional love, likewise, has its nemesis in annihilation. Here the condition of seeking to hold on to that which we think is the "final frontier" before dissolution is the barrier. Beyond that barrier is Supreme Love. No fear and no danger. There you know the unity of all things and that you are ONE. Out of the womb of Supreme Love all is born, and back into that womb all return. Never having left or gone anywhere, we realize that we have participated in a magnificent Dream!

Once you attain the state of liberation from Mass Cultural Hypnosis as expressed through the lower and higher Dreams, you then find that your heart expands to embrace the totality of the boundless Supreme Love. It is at that moment that you dissolve your heart into the Heart and purify the whole world, the whole universe. Think about this. All issues on the planet - all hunger, violence, suffering, disease and more - dissolve the moment you dissolve your attachment to them.

If this "appears" impossible, that is because the mind perceives it as such. The Dream needs to self-propagate and the mind will do whatever is necessary to achieve its objectives. The most powerful tool of the mind in this effort is delusion and false imaginings. Yet when we move beyond the mind's illusions and into the Way of Supreme Love, we attain one of those "nothing" moments. The point of dissolution as the consciousness of trying to accommodate a possibility (healing all) reaches the point of no return. Bingo. It happens, and the Power of Supreme Love reveals miracles. Instant healing. Manifestation of all manner of blessings. It is Supreme Love that manifests, not individual desire. It is Supreme Love that directs and coordinates the entirety of Being. The suspension of the laws of God does not take place, because there are no laws in Unity, and God as defined by humanity ceases to exist. There is only One and no governance to regulate, and/or direct anything into pathways of desired outcomes. Not bad!

14

Start In The Foothills

"Your task is not to seek for love, but merely to seek and find all the barriers within yourself that you have built against it."
Jalal ad-din Rumi

It's story time again. Each year I travel with my wife, Regina, to India. These visits are multi-faceted in that they have business, friendship, spiritual rejuvenation and charity work aspects all rolled into one trip. To say that I love India for all that it offers is without question. It is a great place to challenge all that one holds sacred. I have been travelling to this blessed land for over thirty-five years and have formed deep and cherished friendships there. One of my dear friends had, for years, requested that I join him at a hill station in the foothills of the Himalayas very close to his heart. Though I wanted to share in his love of this place, I had politely declined, repeatedly, due to pressing engagements back home. However, three years ago Regina and I decided it was high time to make the excursion with him, his wife and family - at long last we would experience the tranquility and clear air of this beloved mountain retreat.

Packed up and ready to go, we took the train to Chandigarh and then travelled onwards, up the steep inclines, to the old

British hill station of Kasauli. Part of my general reluctance to travel with friends to places where they have a social network reflects my desire to avoid involvement in excessive discourse when I need to recharge my batteries for other commitments. My friend understood this and gave me an ironclad guarantee that our visit would be peaceful and uninterrupted, since few visitors would be present in the village at that time, and if they were he was almost certain that none of his own acquaintances would be present during our brief stay. In addition, our cell phones simply did not work there, so we were safe – or so we thought.

Our first glimpse of the majestic mountains, rolling valleys, and beautiful vista over the vast Indo-Gangetic Plain was accompanied by the occasional sound of a Brahmin bull echoing its displeasure at laboring through the fields with a plough on its back. Other than that it truly was peaceful. God's own garden. We were relaxed and all was still and quiet. Yet soon the meditative silence was broken by the startling rattle of a pre-WW2 phone housed somewhere in the stately residence. A servant ran to the phone and delivered news of the caller to our host. I heard my friend speaking with surprise to someone who, from her vista below us down the sloping hillside, had peered upward to notice his imposing presence and our party's arrival. Yes indeed, on that visit to our oasis of solitude, one moment of "coincidence" had brought another Soul, also well known well by our host, to the exact same spot in time and space.

"Coincidence" always works in strange ways. We act surprised when events unfold in this manner, and yet deep down we know that we have really bought tickets to this film, have choreographed its entirety and entered into it much like Alfred Hitchcock did in all his films. Walking through the set we know that we will most certainly be noticed. This is life and that is coincidence, right? Full of "surprises" - and this coincidence was no less than that.

Despite our friend's pleading to be excused from socializing on this visit, and his request for solace and quiet, the caller kindly insisted that he and his wife join her group for at least one drink that evening at the Country Club. He apologized to me and indicated that while he would go, Regina and I certainly need not attend, though we were most welcome. We, "for some reason", chose to join them.

When we arrived at the club we found it nearly empty, true to my friend's earlier insistence that the vicinity would be fairly deserted. We established ourselves in a comfortable corner. Soon after the friend, whom I will call Sunita, arrived, and happy reunion greetings followed. Within a few moments I was introduced to this delightful lady. This is where our story gets interesting. No sooner had I said hello than Sunita's face transformed with a look of shock. She requested that I immediately repeat my introduction. All I had said was a simple, "G'daye Sunita. Nigel Taylor. Nice to meet you," or something to that effect. These few words were all that I needed to say to unleash the forces of coincidence.

"I know that voice," she said. "Speak again", she implored. I did as asked. Sunita gazed at me with a look of combined wonder, disbelief and shock. I began to feel like I was acting out a scene from *Groundhog Day*. "What did you say your name was?" She asked again. I repeated myself once more. "Oh my Gosh! Not Nigel Taylor!" she said, the shock truly hitting her at this point. My friends and I were in our own state of confusion. "Yes," I continued. "That is my name." "Have you read the Secret!?" she gushed in enquiring reply. I hadn't, actually, but indicated that I was indeed aware of the book. She was so excited she could hardly contain herself long enough to explain the cause for her state of awe and disbelief at meeting me in this remote hill station.

This incident provides a perfect example of the play of the Dream and the dance of Supreme Love through our dreaming. Stay with me now, for even though you may have never heard my voice, and you have no idea who I really am, this is *your* "coincidence" too - as you find yourself reading these pages at this exact juncture in your life path. I ask you this: "Is it coincidence that we are here together, or a collapse of time/space?"

Sunita, as it turned out, knew me, but only by my voice. Many years before this meeting in the mountains, she had acquired a copy of a meditation recording that I had produced titled

Romancing The Soul. The journey taken in this meditation is one of deep inner-plane healing. Sunita had used it with benefit many times, long before, but she had misplaced it over the years. At the moment we met face to face, however, there was an event unfolding in her life that caused her to seek out this very meditation for its assistance. Her search took her directly to the hill station where our party was due to arrive at any moment. She had only just come there herself. For although normally resident in Delhi, she realized that the last place she had seen this tape (yes I said "tape"), many moons ago, was up there in her Kasauli home.

She wanted it, so she set off there to find it! Yet to her surprise, in this quiet oasis of peace in the foothills of the top of the world, she found not only the meditation, she found me! She had happened to glance up from the lower reaches of the settlement, through the foliage, and seen our host as he stood out front of his residence. Nice dreaming Sunita.

I believe my host was a little mortified at witnessing this whole episode, and quite concerned that my evening could turn into a counseling session rather than time out in shared relaxation. As it happened, the former did not eventuate, but Sunita did manage to pry me away from the group long enough to seek some advice. Her challenge was tearing at her Soul, and I felt a need to spend a few moments with her to assist in any way I could.

In short, the issue confronting her pertained to a relationship challenge within the family. Her son's wife had basically excommunicated her from the family, and her son appeared powerless to do anything about it. They had at least one child already with whom she had not been allowed to spend time, and at the time her daughter-in-law was pregnant and expecting another baby within days. Sunita was not invited to see them, or the newborn, when he/she arrived into the world. Right up until that meeting in Kasauli, Sunita had a deep tear in her Soul and it was only getting worse with each day. She wanted to know what to do. She wanted to heal the relationship, see her grandchildren, and move on.

My advice to her was simple. I knew that she would follow

it and I also knew that she would put her heart and Soul into it, since she had reached a point of no return. The pain of the events was more than she could handle. Hence the urgent search for the tape and the joy at our "chance" meeting. I instructed her to go back to her hilltop residence, relax, and engage in the meditation. I advised her to do exactly what it instructed her to do on the inner planes of her Being. Furthermore, I instructed her to go deep inside her Soul, bypass her personality and all the paraphernalia of the lower Dream, and open her own heart to the heart of her daughter-in-law. The remaining details of the story are very personal, so I won't share them, but the key to this tale, and what it helps us to understand about the Dream and the Power Before Thought, lies in the path Sunita followed to heal the issue before her and the pain in her heart.

Sunita had to bypass the lower Dream and delusion of separation of time and space. She had to *yearn* for a resolution (which she did already, hence her journey to Kasauli). She had to accept the play of the Supreme Love as it played out. No judgments, just acceptance. She had to discern the deepest feelings surrounding her part in this play. Then, to heal it all, she had to *let it go*. She assured me that she most certainly would follow the guidance and the meditation process, to the letter. We said good-bye and went home. For my part, the work was done.

The next morning, as we were getting ready to depart (I know, a short visit), the old reliable pre-WW2 phone once again rattled itself nearly off the cliff face. Our host answered the phone, and with a look of surprise on his face peered over to me. "Sunita is on the phone," he said. "Will you take the call?" I took the phone and heard the joy in Sunita's voice as she shared an experience most instructive to all of us who seek to dream our way back to the Dreamer.

Sunita told me that she had returned home after our meeting and carried out all the instructions to the last detail. After this she had slipped into a peaceful sleep. Just moments before her call to me, Sunita had been awakened from her sleep by the ringing of her own phone. Upon answering it, she heard the voice of her daughter-in-law! It was the first time they had spoken in years. If this alone was not a big enough surprise for her, what followed was beyond her wildest expectations. Her son and daughter-in-law called to invite her to visit with them shortly after the arrival of the new baby. Sunita was, needless to say, delighted with the outcome of her journey of Love, taken through the meditation, which had brought her this release from pain. She felt healed, happy and set ready to go forward. Well done Sunita and thank you, for your experience and your healing reveal so much to us about where we have come to in our exploration to this point and where we go from here.

FOLLOW YOUR HEART

Sunita's story, in its very core, reveals the following:

- Time/space collapse when the Soul is ready to let go of the Dream of separation.
- Hurt is an illusion that can be transformed into wonderful joy.
- Following one's heart to the foothills of life's greatest peaks prepares one to go even higher in the spiritual quest.
- We all seek this higher place of peace in our hearts, and when the time is right we will act to find it.

How does this help us to now take the journey ourselves? What does this alert us to and inform us to be conscious of in order to truly experience the blessings of this path? The answer: Discernment, discernment and more discernment. This is the key. Recall the keys of discernment revealed in Chapter 10. Observe how Sunita's experience reveals them in action. We can see how she applied the first key: *Practice Discernment in Thinking* and watch all that your thoughts give birth to in your Dream. We must learn to stop, look, listen and feel the inner truth from our hearts. To watch them, question them, and know where they are coming from. The heart of Sunita was crying out for transformation. She understood that, and she acted accordingly. Then, that part of her that was set ready to help her heal appeared before her as...yours truly! I am Sunita. She is Nigel. We are one, but this oneness can never be realized without discernment.

We see here how Sunita grabbed this key, and her story illustrates how our application of the first key leads us naturally into the second two keys – to *Question The Master* and to *Challenge the Delusion of Mass Cultural Hypnosis*. After Sunita discerned her thoughts and tracked the situation to its core, she knew what her heart was calling out for, and she acted to pursue that calling. She discarded the old Dream along with the pain, hurt and all the baggage that resided in her Soul and personality. Delusion of separation slipped away. Then she came face to face with her teacher (again, yours truly). At this point she then applied the second discernment key, Question the Master. She tested her teacher in the moment, in this instance me. She did so in that she wanted to see whether or not it was a teaching that would hold true. She applied the teaching and the result was already a forgone conclusion. She used the form that I Am as a Self-reflective mirror to achieve her heart's deepest yearning. Dissolution of separation. Her result was so clear and the healing so complete in the "here and now" that she did not need to do anything further. She did not have any delusions to question and hence in applying the third key, to Challenge the Delusion of Mass Cultural Hypnosis, we can see that Sunita was "in the clear".

To assist you in employing this whole process of discernment with perfect clarity, I will now offer a simple formula which, if you pay careful attention to the details, will propel you forward on your journey. Prepare to depart the foothills – look up into the clear sky, focus on the Sun and hear the silence for these are your best references for engaging the journey.

15

Principle - Channel - Motive

*"Your vision will become clear only when you look into your heart.
Those who look outside, dream. Those who look inside, awaken."*
Carl Jung

If you are not a mathematician, don't worry. The formula which follows is provided merely to keep the good ole left brain happy. For if it is not happy, it starts the process of arguing. Ready? Let's take a look. This is really very simple, and if you work with it, it will always be at the back of your mind as a check mechanism to serve you along the Way.

$$3 + 3 + 3 + 1 = 10 = 1 + 0 = \text{Unity}$$

While the left part of your brain plays with the formula, let's get on with the journey of understanding this formula and how it can assist us on the way. But first, let us take an excursion into the world of the ancients and discover how and why formula and the language of number and symbol are so powerful to our understanding of all creation inside the Dream and the Way to follow.

114

THE LANGUAGE OF THE DREAM

There is a core principle central to all mystery traditions. It is the understanding that the Universe (Dream) is explainable at a very high level through the use of numbers. Numbers, as used today in mathematics and all the sciences that have developed forth from this art, have a much greater role to play in explaining the

Dream. They may appear to be simple symbols, as taught in all grades of education with varying degrees of complexity. Yet they are so much more. In fact, to the ancients, numbers were the true Universal language, one that could be used to explain most, if not everything, in the Dream, with the exception of that which comes before the Dream.

The ancients knew that which came before the Dream was existence-less, empty, a void, and yet full, complete and self-sustaining. To this they ascribed the symbol of a circle - representing the never-ending cycle of continuous existence without the need for our Dream. This, some of you may recognize, represents the journey of the Fool in the Tarot deck. He who has completed his journey of life and returns to the vista of a higher mount, looking out with wisdom gained, over the next cycle of his never-ending journey. He is wise to those who are following, and sometimes a Fool to those who he is following into greater wisdom. Yet he is perfect. (He sounds a little like my friendly pooch and his journeys of travel up and down the street.) We are all the Fool, as we are all the characters of each aspect of the journey the Fool engages along the way. We adopt each personae of each character and live out of this immense expanse of Being. Yet, there is that which brings forth the Fool - and communicating this point was the ancients' deepest wish.

Many are those who will stop at the circle, or our zero, and live out of the belief that it truly does indeed represent nothing. This belief is part of the Mass Cultural Hypnosis. Yet, deeper and more fully aware are those that actually surrender to the nothingness that precedes the 1, and enter into the emptiness that is the nothingness or zero. It takes courage and few are those who are willing at any moment to be the Way Showers. These we call Avatars, saints and sages. To these beings comes dissolution and total mergence into that which cannot be spoken of, talked about or even experienced, but by the references of the Dream itself. For the Dream, as you well know, is a construct, built, or engineered, through the use of sacred light and sound with the force of thought. These light and sound frequencies first align themselves into a relationship that delineates the beginnings of possible creation. These can be noted as a prescription, or formulae, for what shall follow. Out of these prescriptive formulae are birthed high ideas, all from the 1. These we call laws, for they dictate the very manner in which they themselves have come into being.

Out of these primary laws emanate sacred geometric forms through which creation then comes into being. These forms move comfortably through the cyclical expanse of the zero birthing the (1) one, which splits into duality and births the (2) two, which further divides into the (3) three, and onwards through to the (9) nine. It is at this point that we reach the (10) tenth expression of Creation by way of these sacred numbers. The 10, being a combination of the 1 and 0, is mathematically equal to 1. We are being told something very simple, and this is that the ten symbols fold back upon themselves and create a new level of existence. All laws come from the 1. Understand these laws and you shall, with relative ease, return back to the 1. This sounds very much like the journey of our lives, and as a result many esoteric sciences have cropped up inside the Dream and used these symbols to explain qualities of Being, aspects of the timing of the journey, and Soul characteristics. They are not final, nor definitive, but they do point the way. The way, though, to what?

With each symbol, or number, inside the Dream, and all combinations thereof - i.e. 11, 328 or 10x10x10x10 ad infinitum - the mystics associated specific attachments, or energies. Your bank account is one such expression of a holding pattern for energy. It has a number, and a series of entries that reveal your assets. Energy. Understand these principles and there is a flow of abundance, or a lock of poverty, that reveals itself to you in the

Dream. These symbolic energies are what we use as the creative ingredients in our recipe of creation. If we live at the lower end of the vibratory scale, wrapped in Maya and Mass Cultural Hypnosis, we reproduce the recipes that we are being fed by media and through other mediums. Fear, anger, judgment, and a lesser love. If we detach from these lower vibratory thought patterns and elevate ourselves up through the cycles of perception to a higher level of being, we start to create from the higher recipes. These are the formulae for greater wisdom, love and light.

To work in the latter manner we become like the Fool, learning to disengage and detach from the thoughtforms that hold us back and keep us in the loop of suffering and pain. This whole journey can be seen in the light of our earlier exploration of the Vehicles of Consciousness. That which is before the Dream is unknown and yet powers the Dream into existence. The Dream is birthed and constructed out of the Power Before Thought. This is the primal thought of Love which is what we believe within the Dream to be the Source, or Divine Light. This is what comes out of the Void, or the nothingness. It is NOT what is in the void. It takes its existence by powering up the essence of the Dream. It is formless and timeless. It is Light, but not as we know it. It is not five sensory light, but rather a Light that is beyond the perception of the mind. It is yoked to the Power from which it was itself birthed and acts as a magnet to attract us back along the Way.

This is the Theos through which the Divine Spark expresses itself. As the unfolding of the Light (in a timeless manner) occurs, then the gradation of energy leads us to patterns of light, ratio, symbol, and structures of possibility. This is the beginning of the vehicle of Spirit as it plays out in the dimension of the Dream we call the Logos. Here we have formulae expressing themselves as the sacred numbers (being sentient and alive) working together to bring forth something beautiful. Formulae at all levels do birth outcomes – think about equations that power your computer!

This creative expression then unfolds like the petals of a rose as it greets the morning Sun, revealing the essence of form. These forms are then further structured into patterns and ideas of being. We call this the realm of formation and the collective of these thoughts and ideas are what we call myth. The myth then is expressed in the realm of function where the formless, through the formulae, into the form becomes expressed in time and space through the world of ethics and personality.

Remember, this is a model, as are the numbers inside the Dream, which assists our understanding of ourselves. The point here is that the ancients knew and studied the spectrum of light from Source through to behavior at the earthly level. From that study and perception came forth guidance that would reveal to us how to move through the angst of the physical attachments and into the deeply peaceful realization of our beingness. For this they took behavior, and recommended specific approaches to breaking through the personality, merging the personality with the Soul. At that point they could then listen to the fallacy of the myth we were living out of and monitor the way we had surrendered to a lesser Dream and a myth that failed to reveal Truth.

Once there they did not stop, for they guided us back higher into our Spirit by showing us how we could cross time and space with our minds when we were free and unshackled from the lower thoughtforms. This they showed by way of formulae that worked repeatedly over time. These were laws, not just any laws but certainly laws that were higher than those man-made. They also knew that these laws would themselves dissolve when they served no further purpose, because they were, in and of themselves, no more than constructs of the Dream. It was through these formulae, however, that we were able to disassociate from the form and go back into the formless, with our awareness of Being in place. Not bad, to know who we are and what we are. To be in the world but not of the world. But we mustn't stop here - for there is more!

There is the step that takes us through the circle into the pre-Dream state. This is beyond the power of thought to the Power that precedes thought. Many are called and few succeed. You are one of them, or you would not have come this far! There is work to do, but it is worth every moment of your time, which of course is an illusion, so let's not be too attached to that! This Power we have identified not as love, but as Supreme Love, and yet even that is not enough. For if we can define it, we have not truly experienced it. Hence we use words here only as guide posts along the way. Use them in that way only, no more. Let us now let go of the serious side of being for a moment and enjoy what follows. If you follow me in a spirit of joyful Self-enquiry, your results will hasten and multiply in terms of the highest rewards.

FROM FORMULA TO FORMLESS

Let us delve into our formula, strengthened by our knowledge and understanding of the language of number and symbol. We can see now how effectively formulae helps us along our journey on the Way of Supreme Love. The use of formula is not done for the purposes of being mathematical, but rather for the purposes of having a focus to always return to. Again, I repeat the formula here before we move into the next chapter and deepen our understanding of its parts and how it guides us along the Way we seek to follow.

$$3 + 3 + 3 + 1 = 10 = 1 + 0 = \text{Unity}$$

Simply put, there are three *Power Principles*. We will direct our focus on one and the other two will fall in line. Out of this chosen Power Principle emanate three *Energetic Channels* through which we can direct our Dream. We will focus on just one primary channel and again, the other two will fall in line. From this chosen Energetic Channel of consciousness are revealed three *Master Motives* that welcome us to higher reaches of awareness. Again, we will focus on one Master Motive which will bring the other two into abeyance. Taking this chosen principle we then will walk through the flame of attachment to the path itself and unite the blessings that all of our work in the lower levels has poured upon us. This is into the field of Unity. In the field of Unity, the "1" which is the "I", will then be shown how to dissolve itself from even that limiting consciousness and pass through the circle of nothingness into the

Power Before Thought. Getting there is fun, and you have made huge leaps and bounds simply by coming this far! Now it is time to embrace the journey and take it to its rightful place – in the core of your Being. Your heart. The HeartSpace. Beyond Zero Point!

The Power Before
                    Thought

Unlocking The Code

*"Faith is an oasis in the heart which can never
be reached by the caravan of thinking."*
Kahlil Gibran

$$3 + 3 + 3 + 1 = 10 = 1 + 0 \text{ Unity}$$

We begin our journey through the formula with a quick review of what has been revealed in the previous chapters, specifically in Chapter 10, and that which is illustrated beautifully through Sunita's transformative experience. We have already explored the first "3" of our formula, and hence I will not go over them again here, other than to list them. These are the three *Power Principles*. As we have already seen, when we work with the first, the latter two will automatically come into line. They are:

Power Principles : 3

* Practice Discernment in Thinking

* Question the Master

* Challenge the Delusion of Mass Cultural Hypnosis

When we engage these Power Principles, we need to do so in context of three *Energetic Channels*. These three Energetic Channels are born from the Power Principle of discernment and represent the second "3" in our formula. They are:

The Power Before Thought

Energetic Channels: + 3

* Discernment of Deeds.

* Discernment in Meditation

* Discernment through Devotion

Caution! Resist the temptation to enter into the old Dream patterning of what you think these mean and thereby avoid the risk of losing yourself in the delusion of Mass Cultural Hypnosis. Stay with me here; stay in your heart and out of your analytical head, as we explore these three areas of discernment and their importance to us as we engage the Way.

EXPLORING THE ENERGETIC CHANNELS

Discernment of Deeds

Discernment of Deeds calls upon us to look upon every action we engage as having ramifications across all dimensions. Understanding the much-maligned concept of karma is of great aid to us here. Karma simply means action. We cannot be embodied in physical form and not experience karma. Breath is karmic. Cellular activity is karmic. Sleep is karmic. Why? Because everything is an act, and as an act it is karmic (in this definition).

We now know that we exist in *all* dimensions of time and space. Hence, what may be defined inside the Dream as past, present and future is actually a part of who and what we are at the most fundamental level. Hence, there are parts of us that are, in

122

some way, playing out inter-dimensional actions from what we could define to be past, future and parallel existences. Therefore, if everything inside the Dream is birthed through thought, and thought precedes (in its most fundamental sense) action, we need to be very conscious of our actions. Why? Because they will help us *clear the decks of the preceding thoughts that may lead us into the deeper lower Dream.* Watch your thinking! This is vital.

Ask yourself, at all times, "Whose thoughts are these? How do I feel about these thoughts?" Be ever conscious of the potent power of thought in creating outcomes across time and space. This quality of discernment, this *Discernment of Deeds*, frees us from the trappings of many dimensional interferences, including karma. This Principle is a must.

Discernment in Meditation

Discernment in Meditation means the use of meditative practice as we follow the path of Supreme Love to assist us rise above our involvement in the Dream. Meditation assists us to rise above desires. If we desire something then we believe we are separate from it. There is a yoke between the object of desire and the lower self. Desires are fertilizer for the lower Dream. The act of meditation is a powerful tool employed to eliminate thoughts that no longer serve us.

In practicing Discernment in Meditation, you go inward and feel your way through the inner world. As you apply this practice, remember that there are many paths of meditation. Each has its own blessings. Remember that you are the *Observer*. In meditation you observe your thoughts. You do this by learning to track them and work them back to the Source Point – to the point just before the Power Before Thought. Once there you begin the dissolution process. This requires concentrated application of the meditative process, for our thoughts are great distracters and great engineers of delusion.

For our purposes here, and as a brief introduction to this meditative practice and the gift of discernment it bestows upon us through daily usage, meditation can be divided into two forms: Eastern and Western. Eastern meditation is passive, and through deep concentration yokes the mind to that which precedes Zero Point, Source Point, to Supreme Love. It gently coaxes us along the Way. Western meditation works in an active way and uses symbolism drawn from the Dream. In other words, use fire to fight fire. It directs us along a path, structured out of higher-level symbolism, and ultimately leads us to a place where we can let go of thoughts and merge in the place of the dreamless peace of Source.

Both forms of meditation are valid, and both also require discernment of the inner images, feelings, and activities that are birthed from the practice of meditation. The constant pull of mass cultural icons of need, want and desire act as a drag along the path of life. Meditation acts as a potent gift to lead us away from the drag. This also is a must!

Discernment through Devotion

Discernment through Devotion is the application of discernment through our devotion to Supreme Love. I must start by saying that "devotion" is a potent and heavily laden word in the thought streams of mass culture. Yet here I am referring purely to the deep and abiding affection and loyalty to the inner knowing of your heart - the heart that actually knows it is Supreme Love. No more and no less, no filters of meaning or structures of belief involved. How you perceive it is not my concern, as long as you understand the essence of devotion. This *is* my concern.

Careful recognition of the intent behind one's devotion in life can actually override the need to spend a great length of time and mountains of effort dedicated to the former two areas of discernment – of deeds and meditation. It requires no great rigors of the body or Spirit, but it does require an understanding of the way the Dream works.

Discernment through Devotion to Supreme Love asks us to give up all desires and dedicate all actions (i.e. deeds) and all thoughts (i.e. meditation) to the principle of Supreme Love. When you offer every single thought, word and deed to the Supreme Love that precedes the Thought of your Being, this alone becomes an act of devotion to and for that Love. This is an act of offering to the Supreme. Now, I do understand that this might not sit well with those who have had challenges with religion and the like. But this is not religion. It does not require that you believe in any form of religion. *It simply acknowledges that the principle of Supreme Love is that which is at the Source of all that is.* Reaching any religious or metaphysical viewpoint is your choice and yours alone to do, should you choose to, as you unlock the path of devotion. To that end we now unfold the next three aspects of our formula.

The final "3" in our formula represents three *Master Motives* that act as the driving force, the magnetic pull to actually participate in the devotional act itself. These are the master intentions behind our acts of devotion to the Supreme Love. They provide us with the ability to see how the Way is fraught with pitfalls we must avoid, and how discernment, our trusted friend, will lead us through the Dream's delusions to ultimately reach the "1", the One, Supreme Love. These three master Motives are:

Master Motives: + 3

* Devotion for Self Advantage.

* Devotion for Personal Desires.

* Devotion for Purification of Self.

EXPLORING THE MASTER MOTIVES

Devotion for Self Advantage

Devotion for the sake of advancement over another part of oneself in the Dream is a form of devotion that actually inflicts harm. Yes, love can hurt, you have heard that before! We can channel love to bring hurt. But this type of devoted action will, as wise ones know, always return to self like a boomerang. It represents a heavy energy, coloured by a dark ignorance and steeped in a negative understanding of love and the use of love for expansion. Such a path, if followed, leads us to contraction – not expansion. If we choose to think less than loving thoughts, relative to another Soul, to advance our own journeys, we will be sorry. We might as well save ourselves a lot of effort by simply downing a cup of hemlock. For truly, any such thoughts will circle back upon us, because all are *One*. Just One playing out in the Dream as love, protecting itself from the delusion of separation.

This form of devotion to Supreme Love is coloured by the energies of the lower Dream in such a way that it is not *truly* love where the devotion is directed. Since the dawn of civilization, people of the world have prayed to their personal god form to intervene on their behalf to bring forth favorable and desired outcomes. Tribal warriors did it. Modern day presidents do it. Even scientists do it, when they pray to the "great god random" to reveal his secrets from the quantum field. We all do it. Anyone who denies ever having done it is actually doing it as they deny it! Then we pray to the "great god denial" to cover our tracks.

This type of devotion to any form or formless principle will always lead us into a space of separation, just as desire does! "If you do this for me I will do that for you," we bargain. If we do this, our Souls are engaged in a lesser love, because conditions have been placed upon the path. You might argue that it is better to have some kind of devotion than none at all, but this is not so. For in the end, separation breeds the energies of malice, contempt, envy, and rage. It is this result that makes an *absence* of devotion perhaps somewhat more desirable. Recognition of this pitfall along the path is of great import for all who seek the blessings life has to offer. This motivation simply does not produce results no matter which way one views it. There is only ever the consequence of playing at a lower level in the Dream.

Hence today's Mass Cultural Hypnosis propagates a false

argument as to the true nature of our Being. (Here we see the red flag of separation again.) In this false argument, we see one side argue for faith and all of its trappings relative to "whose God is the right God", and we see the other side arguing for no God. A mere glimpse into the Dream of today will bear evidence to this truth. We witness the detrimental effects of this form of devotion in the lower manifest forms of Mass Cultural Hypnosis which pit Christian and Jew against Moslem, and Catholic against Protestant, and Atheist against Believer, and all the variations thereof. We know how this devotion plays out and we, in our hearts, feel the pain of the consequences. Just as Sunita did. It is high time to transform all of these energies.

Devotion for Personal Desires

Devotion for the sake of meeting one's own ends within the lesser Dream is quite easy for most of us to recognize. Within this form of devotion there is no desire that any other should suffer, which often characterizes the first type. Rather, this devotion is simply to meet one's own desires within the Dream. They may be great desires that one wishes to accomplish, associated with pleasure, wealth or achievement. This is a very active, dynamic, and creative form of devotion, and it is distinctly tied to the emotional love of one's purpose-driven reality within the Dream. Devotion and service such as this helps the Soul to remain focussed on the higher love, and yet there is still desire of a lower love that sidetracks them along the path. This love is for the object of accomplishment - i.e. for the achievement and/or fame and fortune that will come with it. We witness this in business, religion, politics, and most areas of enterprise.

Devotion to the way of Supreme Love for the rewards that it brings along the way is enriched with deep desires that yield very little freedom from the Dream. We must recognize whether we are actually working towards Supreme Love for the benefits offered and credentials gained along the way. If we are, this is not going to help us achieve our goal. There may indeed be reward, but we must discern whether the rewards are more significant to us than the Way itself. We must ask if our devotion reflects a wish for wealth, pleasure, achievement, or even simply the desire to feel good about ourselves. These are all part of the self-propagating lower path of the Dream.

This form of devotion may appear as love-directed and beneficial, and if you place a service-oriented Soul alongside a selfish one, then truly their appearance would, to the world, display that the former is in fact acting for the benefit of humanity. Freedom, though, is all in the detail, and the detail is all in discernment. In observing this, we might ask, "Why is the Soul serving? Is there even a faint hint of self-satisfaction in seeing another benefit from his or her service?" If the answer is "Yes", this does not make the service wrong, but it must be seen in context of the higher goal. Self-satisfaction can become a honey trap to the personality and keep the Soul from advancing beyond and into an even higher level of love and service.

In this form of devotion, the idea of service is coloured by the drive to make a difference and to *know* what that difference actually is and has been in one's life. Here, again, we might ask, "Is it not better to make this type of difference, however flawed, than to make no difference at all, sitting idly by watching the world spin on its axis and taking no decisive action to lift a finger to help anyone?" Maybe, but I ask you to remember, we are speaking here about devotion as a pathway towards *rising out of the Dream.* All forms of self-oriented service are, in the end, devotion to a love of life that is not our Source. They reflect a devotion to aspects of the way love expresses itself in the lower Dream. *Our objective is to rise above all these barriers, become the radiant love itself, and shine back from that sacred place upon the paths of all our expressions of Being.*

Devotion for Purification of Self

Devotion to the Supreme Love to cleanse the self is a stable, balanced and pure-oriented approach to experiencing love in the Dream. It conjures up images of the pure-hearted Souls who live in ashrams and spend their days in meditation, praying and seeking to be the perfect expressions of love. Yet I would argue that we are of limited use to creation if we engage solely in this form of devotion. I have observed this type of behavior over the years, and it is sometimes accompanied by a "holier than Thou" belief structure that generates a spiritual hierarchy inside one's being. Not always, but certainly sometimes. The flaw in this devotion becomes clear in light of our understandings gleaned so far. For you see, even these Souls act from the point of separation from that which they worship. If separation exists, then so will all of the issues that surround the multi-dimensional Dream. In this type of devotion, a Soul seeks to literally surrender all aspects of self to the one Supreme Love and yet still experiences this very same Supreme Love as something to aspire to, rather than realizing they are already One with it.

No true freedom comes from serving creation this way. For as we see, even devotion and service that seeks to purify by relinquishing attachments creates a challenge inside the Dream. "How so?" you might ask. Think about this for a moment and the answer is quickly clear. If we seek to purify by surrendering all that we believe we are attached to that blocks our way to Supreme Love, then we have *separation*. In so doing we establish that "there is Supreme Love" and "there is 'us'" – not One! Hence, observe! The Way is fraught with traps of delusion.

Once again, we are wise to remember that discernment is the key. Always apply discernment – in this case, discernment relative to the *nature* of our service is what we must apply in the area of devotion. Devotion to the Way through true service is the door that the key will open. Our discernment will guide us through to this highest form of devotion and to the "1" that is our next piece of formula. It is:

The Master Motive: + 1

 * Unity Consciousness - Devotion of Love for Supreme Love.

EXPLORING DEVOTION OF LOVE FOR SUPREME LOVE

This devotion is the key to Unity and the quality we have worked towards a deep understanding of. It is the Devotion of Love for the sake of the Supreme Love. This is the pure path of devotion. It is the one we grasp through the application of the keys of discernment and the recognition of the pitfalls of flawed forms of devotion. It is one in which the Soul is *absorbed* in love for Supreme Love. Think for a moment of the radiance that would emanate from a being who lives from a space of love-infused devotion. Loosen your mind for a moment and let this thought sink in. If the ultimate "1", or "One", or "I", took voice, it would simply say, "You dissolve in Love for Me. I Am Christ, Buddha, Allah, the Light, and Ein of Kabala. I Am the rock that calls out, 'I Love You'. I Am the rain that shouts 'I Love You.'"

In this form of devotion to Supreme Love, no trace of desire exists for the fruits of any stream of thinking you may engage in - past, present or future. You do not seek freedom or liberation, nor do you seek a friendship with any personal god, goddess, or god form. You do not seek Nirvana. *You seek only to become that Love that is the Mother of the Dreamer. You are not in love with the Way, or its fruits. You ARE the WAY.*

In this state of love-absorbed devotion, when the very thought of this Supreme Love arises within you, your heart wells in ecstasy. You find that you will sing and dance the tones of love in sheer abandon. The torrents of love pour forth from you in ways you could never imagine. You have risen beyond philosophy and the needs of self-preservation. You have died in your heart for it has been consumed by its Source. You have arisen in your own Self-willed union of Being.

Supreme Love lies at the heart of the Dreamer's Dream and all of what we know and create in our Dream. Beyond and Before Thought. It is behind the Zero Point! Without this limitless font of creative Power pouring forth from the Void, there would be no Dream, no game, no play of creation, and, of course, no Dreamer and no "us". This infinite splendor of Supreme Love is beyond the spectrum of what we can think of, period. But we can "think it", *through our hearts,* into all of creation, as "love" in every definable form. So what are the characteristics of this Unity of Consciousness? Let me list some of them here and see if you feel the experience is worth your while!

* You have no trace of desire for the fruits of your activity. This means that you have no attachment to the outcomes of your thoughts, words and deeds.

* You are not seeking liberation for yourself.

* You want to serve only Supreme Love.

* You see Supreme Love in all things, all times, everywhere. The stones sing, the flowers dance, the Earth plays and the sky guides you from the beacon of Love in your heart.

* The radiance in your being ignites tears of joy from your mortal frame every time you enter the temple of another's expansive love. The tears are not salty but rather sweet. They emanate not from your eyes but from your heart. It is the nectar of Bliss – the Amrit of the Gods.

* Your life is sage and serene.

* All events arise before you, pass through you and leave you – you are unperturbed and unhindered in the knowledge of your inner truth, Supreme Love.

* You are not concerned with the preservation of your body and mind – least of all your mind!

* You have no philosophy to defend. The sense of ego-self has passed through the realm of the heart and dissolved into the Supreme.

$10 = 1 + 0 = Unity$

The 10 becomes the 1 plus 0, and this becomes simply the 1 - Unity. That which we truly are and the Supreme Love which resides in our hearts, before each thoughtform, and in each creative aspect of the Dream. It can be truly said that heat dwells in the fire and that the two are inseparable. Likewise, true knowledge dwells in the human heart and the two are inseparable.

This is the point to which all that we have spoken of has taken us. Think back over the pages of our journey - our exploration of what it is to be Human and the experience of being Self-reflective. Here is the true Self-reflective joy. Knowing this Truth does not eliminate the opportunity to achieve so much in this life, to truly make a difference. It does, however, offer you a Way to attain that greatest place of peace through which you act as the instrument, not the doer, of all thoughts and deeds. Can you allow yourself to go there? Into the Unity of Supreme Love that you are? Are you ready? If so, here are some words to help guide you along the Way. We will explore how they align our Dream with the Great Work and Greater Good as we continue our journey.

Love is my form
Truth is my breath
Bliss is my food
My life is my message
Expansion is my life
No reason for love
No season for love
No birth
No death

V

The Call Supreme

17

Dancing In The Dream

"Myths are public dreams, dreams are private myths."
Joseph Campbell

LOVE IS MY FORM

In Supreme Love, all vehicles in the Dream – your own and all that you have created, dissolve into One. That One becomes the sole vehicle through which creation can now progress in your newly activated Dream. *This sole vehicle is the vehicle of Supreme Love. Supreme Love is every manifest and unmanifest form, formulae, and formless possibility.* There is no such thing as *not being* Supreme Love. Now things get really fascinating and well worth the path to get here! You are One with all. There is no separation, no division, no judgment, and no consequences to flow from them. There is One form - Supreme Love. As we have stated, it is a Love that has no attachments to any drama, relationship, goal, purpose or creed. It has one sole purpose - the expansion of Self.

To expand, the One Self splits into numerous aspects and plays infinite games of "hide and seek" as it endeavors to find new ways of Being. Still One, the Self knows that it is Supreme Love. Supreme Love is Its form. In realizing this grace-filled state you are also aware that you have *not* left this "life", as you know it. You have the knowing, however, that your form of Supreme Love is expressing itself through a physical, emotional, mental and spiritual frame. This physical vehicle experiences all of its aspects as variations of the One form. Unity in diversity. One Self. One Love. One form. The form of the pulse of a higher Truth. All thought becomes empowered towards the highest expression, as you now consciously infuse each and every thought you have, or encounter, with the radiance of Supreme Love. Thus you transform what has been and create anew from a higher vibration. This expression reflects the Light of the One rather than the lesser light of the Dream.

With this One form of Supreme Love comes the knowledge that all things are possible. Space and time warp and weave to accomplish your will. This dance of time and space is the substance of the miracles you so deeply desired in the Dream. Such shape shifting and creation is the art and craft of the "magus". The magician is one who knows how to control the elements inside the suggestion of a Dream they know is not real. When you understand that Supreme Love is your form, and also the form that the elements take in all creative expressions, then you become the magus. Yet as the magus working with the power of Supreme Love, you create from the Unified Field of heart magic, rather than within the duality of lower magic, built on psychic egotism. You bring unity to all that seeks trans-formation. You bring integrity to the field of light that you have expressed through infinite aspects of your Self.

How this is done is not only magical, it is mystical. The mystic explores the grandeur of creation and seeks always to climb a never-ending ladder of Love to higher realms of Light. The magician within you works from the Self-realized personae. You know you are Love, and you seek to bring down the Greater Good into all aspects of being. The mystical magus knows, without doubt, that *Love is Selflessness*, and *selfishness is lovelessness*. You are consumed with the ecstatic pouring forth of this Love into every vibration of the universe. You are the ultimate transformer of all things vibrating at less than the Supreme.

TRUTH IS MY BREATH

There is an enormous gift encoded in the second line of the master's mantra. "Truth is my breath." Truth is your breath. Just think of this in context of all that we have spoken of. What is Truth? We could argue this point from here to kingdom come, or until hell freezes over. (Both of which are merely suggestions in the Dream!) There are infinite little truths, but the highest of all truths can never be spoken. It is the Being that reveals the highest Truth. Every breath you take is a key to building the form of Love that is your vehicle of Truth. Think carefully now and you will quickly engage a great secret. Every breath is coordinated by the needs of the Vehicle of your Physical Body. These needs are in alignment with the Soul's desire to expand and the Spirit's alignment with its higher Being. As long as Love finds a place in your heart, breath will flow. Each breath is coloured by the very thoughts that you hold, consciously or unconsciously, along the Way.

Vedic Indian thought informs us that each Soul, in each incarnation, is blessed with a specific number of words, breaths, and heartbeats. A thought lies behind our every breath. This thought is Pure - it is Love, and it is unsullied by the matrix of the Dream. Only when the lower vibrational frequencies of fear, separation, guilt, judgment, and the like creep in does our heart beat out of peace. If this occurs, lower level thoughts take root there. Our Physical Body makes adaptations to these thoughtforms of fear, pain, and hurt, and we then encode our physical and emotional dreams with distortions to the pure light that we are.

If you hold close the knowing that Truth is your breath, you will hold true always to your Supreme mergence with the Source of Love. This is your Truth. It goes beyond right and wrong, beyond religion and science, beyond all thoughts that construct the Dream. Once known it can never be ignored. Truth is your breath. You breathe unity, non-violence, peace, equanimity, and righteousness with every inhalation. As you breath what is pure, all cellular structures are uplifted and encoded with joy and expansion, and this leads you to life! Health is not a possibility, it is a reality. Remember, if you are ONE with all, then you cannot conceal anything from any aspect of yourself. Yourself knows all. To think, act, speak or breathe a lie, in any way, is to lie to yourself through the multiple aspects that define your Dream. Don't do it!

v

The Call Supreme

BLISS IS MY FOOD

Life is made possible because that which you consume is nutrition for the total Being. The Dreamer knows, and always has known, that Bliss is your food. Bliss is beyond "being happy". It is a state of Being in which all contrasts have dissolved. It is the state of Being that is the Dreamer Him/HerSelf. It is the essence of Being. It is Pure Knowledge of existence as subject without object. It is Supreme Unity and is the essence by which the entire Dream is sustained. It is the nectar that is gifted from the Supreme Love. Bliss is your food in that your feast of Supreme joy requires no miracles, no magic, and no mystery. It requires only the absolute realization that all of creation pulses through your very Being. Light pulses through you as eternal joy and you birth constantly from that place of peace and harmony.

MY LIFE IS MY MESSAGE, EXPANSION IS MY LIFE

Your life is sustained simultaneously in all dimensions. Your multi-dimensional beingness informs all of creation by way of the life that you choose to lead. Your life, in this dimension of time and space, choreographed as it is through Love, Truth and Bliss, is your message. Since you are not any of your vehicles and yet you create and inhabit all of them, and since you are not separate but reside in the hearts of all, every thought, word and deed is a message unto all other parts of your beingness - namely all other "illusionary individuals" in your Dream. This brings enormous grace to those parts of you who consciously know of themselves as residing within you. Their comfort at this truth brings a radiance of light into their lives and they start to merge into your HeartSpace as being One. They expand in their Self-realization and journey forth, readying themselves to cross the threshold and enter the state of grace where you already exist. They are being called back, across a time and space that really never has existed. Expansion is your life! Transformation occurs in the entirety that is your Dream. There is no more a question of free will. This disappeared long ago.

You, at all levels of the Dream, have free will to do as you please. Free will brings with it consequences. These consequences are balances and checks that we put in place to keep the Dream unfolding harmoniously. The play of illusionary laws that govern the Dream. As we progress through the dimensions to a higher level, *we eventually realize that the free will we thought we had is actually the will of the One*. Because there was no separation, there was likewise no choice for decisions to be made that would involve will. As the One there is no choice. There simply is, and this is to Be. This is a great place to be. Ultimately, you realize that the Dream itself is unreal and that you have been dreaming the unreal as if it were real. There is none more powerful and none more free than Thee! In the words of a now timeless prayer, "May Thy will be done." *Thy* is a personality implication which again limits us to stay within the Dream. When we surrender the attribute of Thy to that of the Supreme Love, containing the Omniscient, Omnipotent and Omnipresent qualities of Being, then all we are doing is moving away from resistance to the flow of the Power and into alignment with the transforming potency that is the will of Our One being.

Expansion is no longer hindered by the false premise that one can actually do anything wrong to hurt another. One can only limit the expansion of his or her own life. Forgiveness is an illusion, but one played out with such deep conviction in the Dream. "Forgiveness of who and for what?" we must ask. When we realize that we are One with all, then as the One nobody is separate and therefore nobody did anything to hurt any other! If this is the case, there is no one else to forgive for anything because things and people happen in time and space. You are above all of these and realize that only by playing the game of life can you establish the mass hypnotic belief that you were ever hurt by any one else. It is a fruitless exercise. Why? Because this is your Dream and your Dream fills the field of beingness to create magic, mastery and mystery in your One life. Forgiveness is only of self to Self. Since Self is One, we forgive the lesser love within for helping to cloud the greater Love that is. No more. Transform self, expand life, and heal the Dream.

NO REASON FOR LOVE, NO SEASON FOR LOVE, NO BIRTH, NO DEATH

Operating from the point of Oneness with the Dreamer, at all times in all places you are Supreme Love. There is no rationale or division between one Soul aspect and another, no judgment, and therefore no past, present and future upon which to base judgments. Without this energy you are free to simply Be. Hence there is no reason for Love. Love is! Since Love is, you quickly realize that it always has been, as have you, the Ultimate Source of Love. There is no time for, and therefore no season for, Love. The Dreamer is time and yet also above time. Seasons, the ebb and flow of the currents of life hold no sway over the essence of your Source. Supreme Love never dies and is never born, it is timeless. Hence there is no birth and no death. It is this latter realization that frees you, and all aspects of your Self, along the journey of Self-realization. There is no fear when one knows this state of Being. Fear works as the nemesis of a less than pure love. It hides in the shadows of past, present and future unknowns. Without these artificial divisions there can be no fear.

In this unified state of Being, you - as the One - realize that you have a mission to accomplish. A mission that is joy filled and yet still a challenge. For you to create all that you desire, to manifest all that is in your "yet to be thought into being" Pure Heart, you must first empty your "ancient heart" of all that in any way encumbers your journey. Any shadows that block the light of your Soul from shining through must be removed. This is simply a matter of will, activated from your vantage point as the Power Before Thought, as Supreme Love.

The key to this task is to apply a powerful cleansing "filter" to all aspects of your Dream. You must absorb back into your Self all parts of the Dream that do not bring Bliss to any aspect of the created. This point is very important: *All parts of the Dream which do not support Bliss.* Remember, Bliss is your food. To engage this task, which is in itself a moment by moment engagement as you travel through the ocean of your experience, you must ensure that you support yourself first with the sustenance you will need. You do this by cultivating the Truth. This unlocks the door of Love and your life then merges in that supreme state of Being.

The Light In The Looking Glass

"Stop thinking and end your problems."
Lao Tzu

THE ALL INCLUSIVE VERSUS THE MUTUALLY EXCLUSIVE

Supreme Love filters through all dimensions into all Vehicles of Consciousness. It is radiant, not projected nor linked. It is life enhancing, life changing and the Source of all that is. It is the Power to transmute all thought into Pure Thought and all Pure Thought back into that which precedes it - being itself Supreme Love! You are, by nature, the Greater Good that you seek to bring forth. To do any less is to surrender to the forces of Mass Cultural Hypnosis. Supreme Love is literally Omniscient, Omnipotent and Omnipresent. It is our preoccupation with being a physical, emotional and mental Human that causes this magnificent quality of Being to recede into the hidden depths of our Dream.

When we understand, through genuine Self-reflection, that there is only One, we can finally understand that unlike the individual Human with one brain, two eyes, and one stream of thought, the Power Before Thought is profound. This Power is the Source of *all thought*, manifest and unmanifest. It contains all eyes, all brains and all feelings - before, during and after manifestation. Supreme Love is by definition all that is. It is inclusive, all encompassing and, as a result, without judgment and separation. Hence no fear. With no fear comes no battle and no illusion. Humanity, on the other hand, can only think in the mutually exclusive manner of separation, and in so doing it separates by default one aspect of observation from all other aspects. It is a self-creating and, at the same time, Self-denying play inside the Dream.

ENLIGHTENMENT FOR ALL

You now know you are, in and of your Self, the Power. With this knowing comes the understanding of how to change your reality as a multi-dimensional being, unfettered by time/space and the structures of the lesser Dream. You have the ability and knowing of how to change your Dream which, if practiced consciously and with great intent, will yield a reality for yourself that is more profound and beautiful than you could imagine. Using the fullness of the Power Before Thought to change the Dream as we have known it, for Self, also changes the Dream for all. Remember Tesla's comment as to the power of just one thought of a tyrant. You are hardly a tyrant, and yet you have access to the exact same Power. How do we apply this filter?

How do you know you are "getting there" in your re-creation process? In what follows we offer suggestions – again, all are suggestions, nothing fixed, and all pliable for re-creation in your Dream – that you can work with as you dream your way back to the Dreamer and then into the Dreamer's Mother's Heart. *Yes, the Mother principle is the Womb that is the Dreamer Himself.* They are inseparable Mother/Father, Dream/Dreaming, and Power/Power in Action. To give you a taste for what will unfold as you engage the Way, let us take the first step together to reveal a little of what is to come!

Using this simple practice you will know and feel - through your HeartSpace - that the shift in your Dream has begun. Journey with me through this powerful re-creation process, with intent and love-directed will, and watch the purity shine through your heart and Soul. Watch how your Dream and the Dream of all the 7 billion aspects of your Self change. For remember, when you change the thoughtforms of reality, you change them for ONE and ALL. What you experience as you engage the short journey below will offer you a brief but awareness-generating insight into the great possibilities latent within your creation as you pass through the Ten Doors of the Heart, the suggested process of transmutation which completes our journey together in this adventure of the Power Before Thought. Acting as the Dreamer's instrument of Supreme Love you will have the opportunity to embrace these Ten Doors and the Way beyond the Dream.

This glimpse to follow is only intended for you to start the journey and feel the initial shift in your reality it will bring. Before you engage it, take the time to find a place of stillness. Somewhere you can and will relax. You may choose to have someone read this to you, or read it on to a recorder and play it back. If you do, tone and pace yourself. There is no rush. This is just the beginning! (Alternatively, you can visit our Home site for a full range of meditations, including the entire Master's Heart Series).

A GLIMPSE THROUGH THE VEIL

Begin by making yourself comfortable, hands and legs uncrossed, sitting or reclining is fine.

Now, take a few deep breaths and feel your whole Being unwind into a peaceful stillness, fully present in this moment. Just take a few moments to truly be in this space. Quieten the mind. Still the thoughts. Close your eyes.
Bring your awareness to your HeartSpace – bring your focus away from your mind and into your feeling center. Feel centered in yourself,

however that might feel for you.

Now fill that center of yourself, your Heart center, with feelings of love. Use whatever images or thoughts that come to mind that you associate with the deep feeling of love.

Now imagine that this love is like the Sun in your being. It is warm and the light from this Sun is strong and soothing. Focus on the Sun.

Expand this Sun from your Being out into the space around you, in all directions. Sense it. Feel it. Know it. Be free of assessment and judgment, and then expand it further to the world around you and into the infinite space around you. You now have the Sun within you and around you. It is part of you and extends beyond you, encompassing all upon which its rays fall.

Now feel the warmth of this Sun of Love. The Love feeling has grown and expanded beyond your personal love and into an all inclusive Love, flowing out as rays of light into every atom of your Being and into the space around you and beyond into the universe. Breathe in and feel this Light and Love in every atom, of every atom, of every atom of your entire multi-dimensional being. And then deeper.

This Sun within your Heart is the Sun of the One Source of all, the Dreamer's Supreme Love. You are not separate from this Light and Love, you are the embodiment of Supreme Love and you hold the Power Before Thought within you to change your Dream through weaving this Love into all of creation.

While now in this space of feeling Love and Light, within and encompassing you and all, think about anything in the Dream that causes you to move, energetically, away from the Supreme state of Love and Peace that is your true nature and residence as One with the Dreamer.

These thoughts can be about anything at all that comes up for you.

144

Keep exploring these parts of the Dream more deeply and keep bringing them up into your awareness as you continue to bathe in the Love and Peace of the Sun of your Heart. Breathe with this awareness. Become as the Observer to your stream of consciousness.

Thoughts, for instance, of hunger, starvation, poverty, corruption, violence, war, greed and disease…may arise. Keep them coming, regardless of their source, and continue to raise them into your awareness. They cannot harm you. Give them no power for they belong to the lesser Dream. They are not the radiance that you are.

Now, hold these images, these thoughts, and the feelings they generate within you, in front of your Being, in front of your Heart center and the Sun that is in your Heart, which shines out in all directions. They cannot harm you. Let them take form as a sphere of light that holds the energy they encompass.

Consider now how these are all but suggestions in the Dream, and yet they are having an impact on your Dream. Continue to collect them all before you as you observe them from this space of Love. Become a magnet. Let them come forth and into the sphere before you.

Watch as the rays of your Heart's Sun, filled with Love, become as bright as 1000 suns and the warmth from the Sun increases. It is comfortable but powerfully bright and warm.

Now, through an act of intent and directed will, take a deep breath and breathe all of the collected thoughtforms back and into your Being, into the Sun in your Heart. Pull all of the collected images and thoughtforms into your Being and offer them, surrender them, to the Source of all – to the Supreme Love that lights your Heart and is the Sun that shines within and beyond you. Be at peace. Let them in.

Watch as the brilliant rays of the Sun and your Love envelope these thoughtforms as you draw them into your Being and surrender them, through your Heart, back to your Heart, as One with the Dreamer's

Heart and the Source of Supreme Love that manifests all of creation. Let these all transform into a deep feeling of peace within. Own this now.

In that place of peace breathe out Light and Love from your heart into all directions of Creation. Let these rays shine forth brilliantly so as to fill Creation with Light. Know that you have acted as a Transmuter of great potency. Just reflect for one moment on how powerful this action would be if every Soul aspect in Creation followed your lead. And they can. And they will. All in good time. Which is the time that your Soul is preparing to experience. Open your eyes.

You have been the instrument to cleanse these thoughtforms, these suggestions of separation within the Dream, through your Love-directed will. You have, through directing their surrender unto the Supreme Love of the Heart, acted as the instrument for the transmutation of these energies and the uplifting of the Dream to a higher level. Well done!

This is such a simple yet gentle first step along the path you have chosen to engage. You will feel this in your Being. It may be a subtle feeling or it may be strong. There has been a shift in the Dream through your love and service. You cannot help but be different now from when you started the journey, if for no other reason than certain thoughts had to pass through your stream of consciousness. The more you practice this, the stronger the feelings will become, and you will know that what you are doing is truly shifting reality.

Note that there is a reality tone to your journey. For what are thoughtforms? Real forces. In the point of Source, in your heart, you can transmute them and surrender them back to the Light that is your core. Your HeartSpace. By performing this act of service on a daily basis, and doing so with an ever-increasing willingness to penetrate to the deepest parts of Being, you will heal not only your own Dream but also the Dream of all those with whom you share. This is the message of our time. It is the key to open the door to a new age of great joy.

146

Ten Doors Through The Heart

"The Earth Would Die If The Sun Stopped Kissing Her."
Hafiz

I SEE THE LIGHT

When I started to bring this book together I had one objective in mind. I wanted to slice through the mass of ideas that fill the spiritual arena today and create a practical approach to cutting through the trappings of the Dream. The result was to be, for those who chose to work with this material, a place of clarity and integrity in their Being. A place from which they could then discern, from the great array of possibilities, exactly what they wanted to do within the Dream and how they could best accomplish this.

I have been teaching for forty years (I started as a trainee teacher at age 17) and can honestly say I have seen an enormous amount along the path. There have been some magnificent teachers I have brought into my awareness, both from the positive and from the less than positive side of the equation. However, they all taught me to be discerning, and I believe masterful, in my choices of what to follow and what not to follow. Hence, through this book I wanted to help you do the same, because the Mass Cultural Hypnosis we have so frequently referred to also applies to the field of New Age thought.

Any seeker on the path need only spend a few moments exploring the Web to find out that they have a plethora of information to choose from. Literally, the list seems endless, including everything from Mind Power Training, NLP, EFT, Quantum Healing, Aromatherapy, Kinesiology, Astrology, and countless other pathways, not to mention those more deeply sourced from spiritual tradition. Then, born of this expansive list, are infinite practitioners, each with his or her own take on what to do and what not to do. "Confusion" would be a very polite word for that which greets many who are just starting their conscious participation in the journey! It is also possible that one can fall victim to some fundamental errors being prescribed along the way by less than honest practitioners. Here, again, the three Power Principles must play their role.

Having said all of this, I want to emphasize that I do not ask, nor recommend, that you take anything I say as absolute, as gospel. It is simply because I, like you, am inside the Dream and I, like you, am talking to myself in writing this material. I am you and you are I. We are one. So what part of you that I Am has brought you to this place of Self-reflection? My words are the teacher within you, and I am speaking to the Power behind the thought of who you believe you are. I am that Power, as are you. Here we commune and here we can make powerful dynamic and magic changes in the field of consciousness that dominates this world.

It is my firm belief that if we could just get enough people to think in new ways, drop their fears and act from the HeartSpace that is the residence of Supreme Love, then war, famine, drought, disease, violence, and all their "children", would actually simply disappear. Yes, once and for all. Gone. Does it sound idyllic? Good, I hope it does, because it if sounds real or delusional then we are not connecting at the level of the heart. So let me tell you one last story before we set up the very simple steps that will assist you to come into this sacred space.

In 2001 I had just returned from Australia where I had been working and visiting my parents and friends. When it came time to depart for the long haul back to the States, I said what I knew in my heart would be my last physical farewell to my father. We embraced and he looked at me in the eyes and told me that he knew in his heart that this would be the last time our eyes would meet. After our loving embrace I said my final farewells, and the long journey back began.

Just two months later, Regina and I were set to embark on a trip to India as escorts for a large group of spiritual seekers. This was post-911. The night before we left for India my mother rang me from Perth to tell me that my father's passing was imminent. She asked me to return home immediately. I wanted to, but I simply could not walk away from a group of 25 people visiting a new land. Unsure what to do I went into the silence. It was in that silence that the one who has always shown Himself to me as the Master appeared. In my Dream, he is my Master. I test and discern every message I receive, and this was one of the most important times to do so. I asked what to do. "Come see me I will take care of your father," were the words. That was my answer and that is what I did.

I asked my mother to get my father to write a letter to the Dreamer, anything he wanted. Then I asked her to fax it to me as soon as she could. In India we led the group to the places we had promised. When there, I held out the message to the living Dreamer, who had guided me throughout my life. He took the letter and without reading it simply said, "Your Father is mine." We all have living Dreamers and we all rely on them to guide us. Not a spirit guide, not a teacher, but a living Master. The issue for most of us is that we have been conditioned to not discern or to accept that this possibility could exist inside Mass Cultural Hypnosis. My Dreamer is not your Dreamer, but you still have one.

Two weeks passed and we returned to the States with the group. Immediately upon our arrival, my mother called to say, "Dad is hanging on, please come home immediately." We did, and

I arrived home in Perth just two days later. I was 15 hours to late, for my father had passed the night before I arrived. What followed is most significant.

Sitting in the small government assistance home with my mother, wife and a friend, we spoke with the funeral home director who was assisting us. He was a also a church minister. I personally did not belong to any path and so welcomed him in the home, for he was the one my mother had chosen. He had only been seated a few minutes when he opened up. He indicated to me that something unique had taken place with the event of my father's passing. The minister had turned up the night before, shortly after my father had passed, and he walked into the bedroom where my father still lay.

The observation he made must be repeated here word for word. He said to us, "I can honestly say I have never, ever in my life been to a house, where someone has passed, in which I have felt such amazing peace. I can also say that never, ever in my life have I seen the departed reveal through their eyes what they experienced as a last breath. I can tell you now, whether you believe me or not, that your father saw God in his last breath." I could say I was surprised, but actually I was not - for two key reasons.

Firstly, my mother and two lifelong friends of ours had been with my father when he took his last breath, and they explained to me, in detail, the last thing he did. He had reached out to the bedside stand and taken a dearly beloved sacred image of Supreme Love to his heart. He held it over his heart, his eyes opened, he looked up, and his last words were, "I see the angels. I see God." His took his last breath, and in peace he crossed dimensions into the Light. Not the light of fear and pain, suffering and despair. The Light of the Love that had guided his entire life.

You see, this first reason I share with you explains the second key reason. My father was a wise old owl. Always was and nothing could shake him from that place, he was not a religious person. He had attended church, but that was more to keep the protocol in place for having children in this society. He did not judge the church, it was just not for him. At the age of 14 my father said to me, "It is now up to you son to decide what you want to do with your life. You can go to church, or not. You can believe whatever is in your heart, but you alone must make these decisions. We will not force you to do anything that is against your deepest wishes." He with my mother told me go and explore. I did and still am. When I started teaching these principles many, many years ago, my father was the first one to smile and encourage me. In fact, it was he who came to my seminars and stood proudly at the back watching his youngest son take people along a path of exploration. He went with them every step of the way. He never faltered and always found a friend to help, in the midst of it all.

So why do I share this with you now? Because it is the story of your life too. Whether you are young or old, healthy or in a health-challenged state, male or female, a spiritual junkie, church or temple-goer, or an atheist, this is your life. In your heart you know you have great freedom to be at peace. You do not have to wait until your last breath. My father did not wait. He lived in a state of constant spiritual awareness. He would often talk to me about the tunnels of light and what he saw. He was excited by all that he experienced in classes and he was excited that even with his minimal resources he could make a difference in his life and the lives of those with whom he shared. Your life is not decided. It is alive and ready to break free from the shackles. It is now possible that you can choose to follow the path I am outlining before you in the following pages. As simple as it may seem, it will produce results. I encourage you to grab the opportunity before you and truly make a difference.

If you engaged the exercise in the last chapter, then you most probably felt something. I do not know what it was. It might have been a little spark of knowing, a flood light of awareness, or an "ah hah" in your Soul. You have tapped on the door of the heart and know now, like it or not, that an immersion back into the fields of Mass Cultural Hypnosis will soon hold no sway over you. You will start to see a bigger picture, and possibly this will cause you to protest that this is not what you signed on for in this life.

Or you may assert that you are not religious. Neither am I. But

I do acknowledge that I belong to something much greater than my personality and that, in itself, is the starting point for getting over ourselves and entering the transformation. You may protest that you just want a miracle. Guess what? You are the miracle! You, when you know who you are, dissolve the laws and structures of time and space. Miracles are not the suspension of God's law but rather the fulfillment of the joy of Being. To some that is the fulfillment of God in their hearts. It doesn't matter if that is not your myth. What matters is that you stretch the boundaries of fate and test the rhythm of creation.

Our age is within the Dream and structured on the suggestion of time. Yet there are no confines of time or space, or of birth or death for the Being or for the Dreamer. There is no beginning or end, there is only now. The looking glass is so much more powerful when *you are the light* shining through the glass. Let not a lesser Dream make you beholden to a lesser love. Reach out and manifest with great abundance and joy – be at peace and watch as the majesty of your highest Dream unfolds before your eyes.

OPENING THE DOORS

Setting up and creating a "protocol" for one to "follow" can be in itself counterproductive. This entire volume has established itself the task of helping free you from a lesser Dream. From fixed suggestions in the Dream. Therefore, while working with *the Ten Doors Through The Heart* that have been drawn from this text and summarized for ease on the journey, I ask you to remember that they are stepping stones derived from within the Dream. I suggest that you follow them as prescribed and experience the freedom as it unfolds. Then it is time to dismiss the steps and become the Being that you are! These doors are no more and no less than simple steps that will redefine your awareness of Self. They do however, produce great good for your Self and all.

How you choose to embrace these steps, and at what pace and depth, is entirely up to you. I can tell you though, if you truly work these possibilities into your life, great abundance of love, light and joy will be revealed. When your Being is enthused with this Supreme Power, it will ignite a life so rich and so deep with the expansiveness of Bliss that nothing will ever step before you to halt your service to the One. Endeavor to work with one step a week and then integrate the second step on top of the previous one, two or three as you progress.

These suggestions for dreaming the new Dream may seem simple to you, almost too easy! "I have heard it all before," you might say. Don't be fooled, however, for as you ask the questions and observe how the answers shift your Being, you will apply the suggestions offered to you throughout this volume and discern your way powerfully through the pathways of the Dream. You have already started to free yourself simply because you have read this book. The journey is underway. Your Self Reflective Consciousness will take you on the journey through your levels of Being and through all dimensions of the Dream upon the Way to Supreme Love. The unfolding of this Love, through all thoughts, deeds and service, done through your Heart at One with this Supreme Love, will change the Dream forever.

Remember, the ultimate secret to undertaking this journey successfully and joyfully is to *stay in the space of your heart – to journey through your HeartSpace as you follow the Way of Supreme Love to its Source.* It is to honor the highest devotion to Supreme Love and to serve from that space as you draw the Power Before Thought into the Dream. Affirm that you will keep the feelings of love and heart-centeredness through every breath, every heartbeat and every word – spoken and unspoken. In this manner you will recreate the Dream by weaving the Power as the most potent force in all Universes, through all levels of your Being, travelling in all of its vehicles through all dimensions of space/time. I will see you in your dreams!

(1) Recognizing The Door

Upon awakening, breathe deeply and slowly for just a few moments. Halt your thinking by becoming the observer of the streams of consciousness that flow before your mind's eye. Then empty your mind by bringing into focus the most joyful thought you can summon up. Ignore "reality". Let that go. Stay with the game. In that space, affirm to yourself: *"Today I search behind my Dream."*

As the day unfolds ask yourself constantly, *"Is this my Dream? Is it someone else's Dream? Am I reacting to reality or living truth?"* As you ask these and all questions suggested in the following steps, do so with awareness and knowing that you are infused with the Love of the One Heart and allow love for Self, and all within the Dream, to be the filter through which your answers arise. Stay in the space of your heart. Do this exercise every day for at least one week. Keep a journal. Join the blog and write your experiences for others to share. There are so many who are on the same path - meet and cross paths with your other aspects.

(2) Turning The Handle

Find a moment to ask yourself the ageless question: *"Who Am I?"* Do not settle for the first answer. Go deep. Do this rather than listening to the car radio, TV, or mindlessly walking around performing a daily chore. When you meet other aspects of Self, ask the same of them, but do so in the inner realm of your Soul. Ask, within your Self, *"Who are you?"* Just keep asking until you get the answer. Do not settle for the mass hypnotic answers of race, creed, culture, age, gender, and so forth. Go deep. Do this frequently during the day. Watch how this deepens your perceptions of everything in your environment.

Monitor what happens to your being. Ask, *"How do I feel as I go deeper and deeper within this question?"* Allow yourself the freedom to expand with the answers, and surrender beliefs and suggestions projected upon you, to find a new pathway through the Dream. Go to the *emptiness* and the *silence* that this process encourages. When you empty that which is full of all that you are not, there is a lot more space to fill with that which you truly are. *Stay in the heart.* Again, do this exercise for at least one week, if not

154

more. Keep a journal and be honest in your reviews. Go back to the blog and share with others.

(3) Opening The Door

Every day take careful note of each event that causes you to experience any emotion whatsoever. Joy, happiness, anger, temptation…through to sadness. Ask yourself, *"What are the thoughtforms (pet dogs) I have following me around today? Are they uplifting my spirit or restraining my joy? Am I my emotions? Am I addicted to these emotions? How do they serve me?"* Then ask, *"Who is the Me that they serve?"* When you look at these emotions, ask to see the clouds they form that are blocking out the light of your Love. You will see how they create limitations within your Dream.

Recognize these clouds and apply the suggestions we have explored. Track your thoughts and feelings to their origin and apply the keys of discernment. Those clouds which are no longer of service to you in the Dream will fall away and be replaced by those which assist you to bring the Power Before Thought to each aspect of your life. Every thought or creation you bring forth will carry Supreme Love into the Dream at all levels. Stay in the heart. Make sure that you journal your answers and do this for at least a week or more. Once again, share in the blog.

(4) Walking Through The Door

Before retiring at night ask yourself one question: *"If I had never been born, how would the world be a different place?"* Be honest and look at everything that would dissolve. Remember, the question is not one of what would happen should you die; it is what would the world be like if you had never been born. Track back from the current moment through the illusion of time and look at how all relationships and circumstances fall away. Keep going back, further and further, until you bypass the point of incarnation. Then ask yourself, *"Who Am I?"* once again. You will observe as the shifts and changes in your Dream occur through this deepening exploration. Stay in the heart. Blog and journal.

(5) Working Inside The Sanctuary

At least three times during each day speak to your DNA. This is the formula through which the form of your love shall pour forth. If you can speak with love and adoration to your DNA then it will *in-form* the myth of your Being to restructure its behavior to accommodate the Supreme Love in your life. Supreme Love then functions in your everyday Ethos, or behaviors. This is a special treat! The more you practice it, the more profound the blessings in your experience will be.

Give commands to your Spirit to create in accord with a higher good - the Greater Good. Think carefully about what codes would have to play out in your life to create any of the physical, emotional, mental, or spiritual challenges you may have already experienced or are experiencing. Then choose to rise above these challenges and script the changes to your DNA. You do this by imagining, visualizing, and affirming a higher Truth. Meditation practice will help you greatly in this process. I have included a special page on the Power Before Thought website to help you understand the many options available with meditation. I highly suggest you consider the details and suggestions given on that page. *As always – stay in the heart.* Journal and blog.

(6) Listening To The Heart

As you go to sleep, complete the following series of questions and exploration. (Do this after following whatever protocol you use for entry into this state of sleep, be it a prayer, a feeling of gratitude, or other process.) Ask yourself, *"Who is God, the Dreamer, the Source, Supreme Love, or the highest point I can imagine?"* Keep asking. Keep peeling back the layers and find the emptiness behind the images the lesser Dream has created. Then drift into healing sleep when your conscious mind gives up.

In the morning when you awaken, recall and note any dreams you may have had during the night. Watch how that which is revealed in the dreams aligns itself with your daily activity that is generated by the previous five steps. Dreams are of vital importance within the Dream. Avoid using the intellect to study your dreams. Drop into your heart and ask to feel their meaning. Again, journal and blog.

(7) Breathing The Doors of All Lives

Spend five minutes, once a day, looking at the images in your life. They may be on TV, billboards, milk cartons, or anything else that you see, it matters not where they are found. Be aware of the connection you have to all of these in the Dream. Some images, as you know, have a greater impact than others, such as television depictions of Human suffering and the like. These are the photographic imprints that link and tie your Soul to the matrix of a lesser Dream. When you encounter them, choose to release them and disengage from their linkage. Then choose a singular image of something which, for you, brings forth the deep feelings of communion and love for something greater than yourself when you gaze upon it. You might choose a sacred image, but just remember to be aware of any "baggage" it might carry, and be careful to discern. Try to find one image that just truly uplifts you.

Note the difference between the images you are exposed to in the Dream and those you choose for their quality of upliftment and love. Notice how they make you feel. Observe how your heart feels either uplifted or depressed by these images. Note those which support expansion and those which support contraction. Of course, as always, stay in the heart. Journal and blog with like minded aspects of Self.

(8) Approaching The Higher Heart

Once a day know that you are living Narada's Dream. Take a deep breath and wait for Krishna's tap on your shoulder. Then get a glass of water, drink it, and laugh at how seriously you have taken your self! Each day, just allow for one tap on the shoulder. It may be literal or metaphoric. Each time it happens, drink a glass of water and then affirm and ask these words, *"Today I search behind my Dream. Is this my Dream? Is it someone else's Dream? Am I reacting to reality or living truth?"* Laugh - and feel your HeartSpace expand. Journal, blog and share.

(9) Opening The Door Within The Door

When engaged in a dialogue with any other part of Self as expressed through 7 billion people on the planet at any time, day or night, become the Observer of your dialogue and ask the following of yourself: *"Am I projecting images upon this Soul aspect? If so, what are the thoughtforms I am projecting? Are they beneficial, and would I want to live out of them myself (as you will)?"*

Simultaneously, become aware of whether you are or are not radiating Love without condition. Just be aware of the difference in these two experiences. No more. Seek to weight your life's interactions more with the latter and less with the former. Enrich your heart with the nutrition of serving for the sake of serving. Serve without attachment to any perceived benefit. Discern this interaction and watch how your HeartSpace expands. Journal, Blog and share.

(10) Leaving The Matrix of Mass Cultural Hypnosis

As the Power of Supreme Love, make it your goal to be the Source point for creating what *lay mentality in the Dream* would call a "miracle" in the lives of at least two people, once a day. This can be very simple. To create a miracle, all you need do is break the hold of the Dream! Suspend the illusion of the lesser law. The rest will follow suit. Do it. You will become addicted to the bliss it brings home to your heart. Then share the bliss with one and all. Someone is waiting for you to be the miracle that *you are*. Journal, blog and share. As you dance the Way of Supreme Love, always remember:

Life is a song - sing it.
Life is a game - play it.
Life is a challenge - meet it.
Life is a dream - realize it.
Life is a sacrifice - offer it.
Life is love - enjoy it.

v

The Call Supreme

About The Author

An "ambassador of the heart," Nigel Taylor has trekked across the planet, working and studying with its vast array of cultures and creeds - from the kabalistic traditions of East and West to the Dreamtime of the aboriginal people of his own land, Australia. He has shared with some of the world's great teachers, from the masters of India to the Bedouins of the Middle East to the Native Americans where he now resides. Guidance received from the inner planes since childhood together with Nigel's life experiences has inspired facilitation of health retreats, shamanistic journeys, corporate spiritual trainings, and his many recorded meditations and books, including *Initiation Into Miracles* and soon to be released *Secrets From The Master's Heart (Volumes 1-6)*. Nigel's work has been covered by national radio and newspapers and endorsed by best selling authors, business leaders, politicians and spiritual seekers worldwide.

In his early teens, Nigel began his first business to assist in the support of his family. He continued this entrepreneurial trend and then trained in Radio and Television and began his own entertainment company. His university education then led him to pursue a career in teaching. Teaching took him to the Australian outback where he shared with and taught Aborigines. He reached a senior position within the Australian educational system before departing on the journey of his present life work. These relationships created a profound spark for his work with the Mind and Spirit.

Speaking directly from the experiences of his own truth, he expresses a love of the Divine, a reverence for the pursuit of truth, a mastery of his path. A visionary teacher, healer, and author, Nigel weaves esoteric and exoteric, ancient and contemporary, to deliver profound truth with a joy and simplicity that makes it fascinating, entertaining, and understandable to all. He has assisted thousands of people towards health, healing, and spiritual understanding, as well as spiritual fulfillment.

To find out more about Nigel and the support materials for this work and all other aspects of Nigel's workshop schedule, visit his authors page at:

www.powerbeforethought.com

OR

For a full range of Transformative Guided Meditations and other support materials visit:

www.nigeltaylor.com
www.nigeltaylor.net
www.thevoiceofmeditation.com

AND

Join Nigel on Facebook
www.facebook.com/thevoiceofmeditation

Made in the USA
Monee, IL
15 May 2023